111 Places in Dublin That You Shouldn't Miss

Photographs by Róisín McNally

emons:

© Emons Verlag GmbH
All rights reserved
All photos © Róisín McNally, except:
Page 123: John Lavery (1856–1941)
The Artist's Studio: Lady Hazel Lavery with her Daughter Alice
and Stepdaughter Eileen, 1910–1913.
Photo © National Gallery of Ireland.
For details of opening hours and events, see www.nationalgallery.ie.
Page 39: © Trustees of the Chester Beatty Library, Dublin.
© cover icon: shutterstock.com / ULKASTUDIO
Design: Eva Kraskes, based on a design
by Lübbeke | Naumann | Thoben
Edited by Katrina Fried
Maps: altancicek.design, www.altancicek.de
Printing and binding: B.O.S.S Medien GmbH, Goch
Printed in Germany 2015
ISBN 978-3-95451-649-0
First edition

Did you enjoy it? Do you want more?
Join us in uncovering new places around the world on:
www.111places.com

Foreword

Contrary to what you may have heard, Dublin is a city where people get straight to the Point. But that's only because "The Point" is a terminus on one of its main tram routes. In most other areas, especially conversation, Dubliners avoid getting to the point any earlier than necessary. They prefer the scenic route.

The Irish capital is a city of storytellers. Indeed, it is seriously overrepresented among winners of that ultimate storytelling award, the Nobel Prize for Literature. Then again, even the city's street signs present at least two versions of everything (one in English, the other – often purporting to be the real truth about a place – in Irish). So it's no surprise the locals can spin a yarn.

In introducing Dublin to the visitor, this guide has also chosen the scenic detour over the main route. It's not that the *Book of Kells*, Guinness Storehouse, Temple Bar, and all the other tourist clichés aren't worth seeing – they are, mostly. But people will find those anyway. For our 111 places, we chose the less obvious sights, or the ones with good, seldom told stories attached.

The list includes, for example, the statue of a revolutionary dog who may have been responsible for the bit that's missing from one of Ireland's most historic flags. It also features the studio of an artist that's a more popular attraction than any of his paintings. And in a city of monuments, it locates the discreet marker – unknown to most Dubliners – of a 130-year-old event still too sensitive for more public commemoration.

Several places in the guide are linked with James Joyce, a writer who didn't win the Nobel, although he's now at least as well known as those who did. Mind you, his greatest book is more famous than read. But to cut a long story short, it's about a man wandering around Dublin. And if you follow this guide, I hope you'll end up knowing at least as much about the city as he did.

111 Places

1 ____ Airfield Farm
Milking the cows in suburbia | 10

2 ____ The Anna Livia Fountain
A sculpture in internal exile | 12

3 ____ The Bernard Shaw Pub
A funky twist on a famous name | 14

4 ____ Bingo at the George
An old game with a new twist | 16

5 ____ Blessington Street Basin
A reservoir that turned into a park | 18

6 ____ Bog Bodies
Silent witnesses to an ancient past | 20

7 ____ Brendan Behan Sculpture
Monument to a writer and jailbird | 22

8 ____ The Brian Boru Harp
Possibly the world's most reproduced instrument | 24

9 ____ Bull Island
An accidental gift to Dublin | 26

10 ____ Bully's Acre
A cemetery with a lively past | 28

11 ____ Burdock's Chip Shop
Dublin's "oldest chipper," but is it the best? | 30

12 ____ Cavendish and Burke Cross
A dark episode in the life of Dublin's biggest park | 32

13 ____ Central Bank Plaza
A popular space under a controversial building | 34

14 ____ The Chapel Royal
Chronicle of a revolution foretold | 36

15 ____ The Chester Beatty Library
Ancient script that made a translator blush | 38

16 ____ The Church
A place of worship to Arthur Guinness | 40

17 ____ Civic Offices on Wood Quay
An epic clash between Dublin old and new | 42

18 ____ Clondalkin's Round Tower
Pieces of ancient Ireland in a modern suburb | 44

19 ___ The Cobblestone
A magnet for musicians | 46

20 ___ Connolly Books & The New Theatre
A haven for radicals in touristy Temple Bar | 48

21 ___ The Countess and Her Dog
A bite-sized story from Ireland's revolution | 50

22 ___ The Croppies' Acre
Tragic past, troubled present | 52

23 ___ Daniel O'Connell's Bullet Holes
Hit in the crossfire of the fight for independence | 54

24 ___ The DART
A scenic rail route with its own accent | 56

25 ___ Door of Reconciliation
Taking a chance for peace | 58

26 ___ Dubh Linn Garden
A semi-secret garden best seen from the air | 60

27 ___ The Dublin Canals
Royal, Grand, and lovely | 62

28 ___ Dublin Doors
Poster-perfect entrances to a Georgian world | 64

29 ___ The Dublin Port Diving Bell
A tiny museum telling an epic tale | 66

30 ___ Dublin Snugs
Secretive drinking in pubs within pubs | 68

31 ___ Dublin's Best Pint
A scientific approach to a long-debated question | 70

32 ___ Dublin's Last Supper
An Irish twist on an Italian classic | 72

33 ___ The Ernest Walton Memorial
Reflecting two sides of a scientific genius | 74

34 ___ Francis Bacon's Studio
A workplace as a work of art | 76

35 ___ The Freemasons Hall
A secretive organisation now partially open to visitors | 78

36 ___ Fusiliers Arch
A gate dividing two traditions of Irish history | 80

37 ___ George's Street Arcade
A haven for Dublin bohemians | 82

38 ___ The Gravediggers Pub
A bar with a passing trade | 84

39 ___ The Great South Wall
A bracing walk into Dublin Bay | 86

40 ___ Hamilton's Equation
One small scratch for man, one giant leap for mathematics | 88

41 ___ The Hellfire Club
A beauty spot with a sinister history | 90

42 ___ Henrietta Street
A riches-to-rags story | 92

43 ___ The "Home" Memorial
A monument to the victims of drugs | 94

44 ___ The House of the Dead
Home to the most famous dinner party in literature | 96

45 ___ The Hungry Tree
Nature's revenge on law libraries | 98

46 ___ The Icon Walk
Reclaiming the back alleys of Temple Bar for art | 100

47 ___ The Irish Camino
Starting gate for an ancient pilgrim route | 102

48 ___ The Irish Jewish Museum
A tiny community that left a big mark | 104

49 ___ The Irish Times Clock
Calling time on Brian O'Nolan's day job | 106

50 ___ The Irish Whiskey Museum
Bottling history | 108

51 ___ The Irish Yeast Company
A shop that didn't rise | 110

52 ___ Isolde's Tower & The Czech Inn
Where the new and old Dublin collide | 112

53 ___ Iveagh Gardens
In the middle of Dublin, but a mystery to most | 114

54 ___ The James Joyce Tower
Built for war, borrowed by literature | 116

55 ___ The Jeanie Johnston
A famine memorial on water | 118

56 ___ Kilmainham Gaol
A prison that became a shrine to Irish freedom | 120

57 ___ Lady Lavery
A beauty who personified Ireland | 122

58 ___ Leinster House
Where the Fighting Irish and the Talking Irish meet | 124

59___ The Liberties
The beating heart of Dublin | 126

60___ The Liffey Boardwalk
A (mostly) pleasant refuge from the traffic-crazed quays | 128

61___ The Little Museum of Dublin
Holding up a small mirror to the city | 130

62___ The Magazine Fort
A 300-year-old ruin that nearly went out with a bang | 132

63___ Margaret Naylor's Grave
The war tragedy of a star-crossed couple | 134

64___ The Marino Casino
An architectural masterpiece in miniature | 136

65___ Marsh's Library
Three centuries of scholarship, occasionally interrupted | 138

66___ McNeill's Pub
A musical twist on the Charge of the Light Brigade | 140

67___ Meath Street
Dear old Dublin at its cheapest | 142

68___ Monkstown Church
A building ahead of its time | 144

69___ Monto
Where Dublin switched off the red light | 146

70___ Mulligans Pub
Where Joyce meets journalism (and journalism wins) | 148

71___ Napoleon's Toothbrush
A brush with greatness | 150

72___ The National Print Museum
Where they mind their p's and q's | 152

73___ Newman House
A clash of cultures on St Stephen's Green | 154

74___ The Old Airport Terminal
A modernist masterpiece and a relic of air travel past | 156

75___ The Old Dublin Lion House
A roaring success story | 158

76___ Oscar Wilde Sculpture
Colourful tribute, geological marvel | 160

77___ Our Lady of Dublin
A medieval statue with a talent for survival | 162

78___ The Palace's Back Room
Inner sanctum of literary Dublin | 164

79   Patrick Kavanagh's Canal Bank Seats
Two commemorations for a poet who only wanted one | 166

80   Phil Lynott Statue
Heavy metal tribute to a rock star | 168

81   The Powerscourt Centre
A once fashionable house, now a house of fashion | 170

82   The Record Tower
Scene of a famous escape | 172

83   The Revenue Museum
The long and painful story of taxation | 174

84   The Royal Irish Academy
Not just for scholars | 176

85   Samuel Beckett's Foxrock
Universal characters, local footprints | 178

86   Shaw's Birthplace
A binman's tribute to genius | 180

87   The Sick & Indigent Roomkeepers Society
A sign of times past | 182

88   Silicon Docks
New technology reviving old Dublin | 184

89   Smithfield Square
Where Cold War Berlin met Dublin | 186

90   Smock Alley Theatre
Dublin's oldest new theatre | 188

91   St Audoen's Anglican Church
An ancient church with a lucky charm | 190

92   St Enda's School
A nursery for rebels | 192

93   St Mary's Chapel of Ease
A church with a dark reputation | 194

94   St Michan's Church
Shaking hands with history | 196

95   St Nicholas of Myra Church
Scene of a Catholic comeback | 198

96   St Patrick's Tower
A windmill at rest | 200

97   St Valentine's Relics
A shrine for young lovers | 202

98   St Werburgh's Church
Ringing bells and fighting fires | 204

99 — Sunlight Chambers
A monument to soap | 206

100 — Sweny's Chemist
Cleaning up after James Joyce | 208

101 — The Táin Mosaic
An epic tale, told in tiles | 210

102 — Thomas Heazle Parke Statue
Lessons in the struggle for survival | 212

103 — Tully Church & High Crosses
Ancient ruins in a leafy suburb | 214

104 — Vico Road, Killiney
The Bay of Naples, Irish-style | 216

105 — Vonolel's Grave
The last resting place of a four-legged war hero | 218

106 — War Memorial Gardens
A memorial belatedly remembered | 220

107 — Wellington Monument
An obelisk with a tall tale | 222

108 — Wild Deer in Phoenix Park
A herd with a long history | 224

109 — Wittgenstein's Step
A refuge for one of the 20th century's great minds | 226

110 — The Wonderful Barn
An otherworldly wonder of 18th-century architecture | 228

111 — Ye Olde Hurdy-Gurdy Museum of Vintage Radio
One man's passion, now an exhibition | 230

1 Airfield Farm

Milking the cows in suburbia

Dundrum is a well-to-do suburb of Dublin these days, but it's not so long since it was a mere village, surrounded by countryside. In the early part of the 20th century there were still many big houses in the area. And among these was the home of the Overends, a wealthy family whose cousins included the president of the Calcutta Stock Exchange.

The last local descendants were two sisters, Letitia and Naomi Overend, who were well known in Dundrum for their love of cars – including a 1927 Rolls Royce – and their ability to fix them when necessary, both having attended courses on maintenance.

But they were also renowned for their Jersey cows, named after characters from Gilbert and Sullivan. And as the city suburbs encroached, making their land ever more valuable, the ageing Overends remained determined to keep their beloved farm out of the hands of developers. The result, in the 1970s, was the creation of a charitable trust to manage their estate as a recreational and educational facility. So when the sisters died, both well into their 90s, the farm lived on.

It was an urban farm by then. And surrounded by housing developments, busy roads, and the revived Harcourt Street railway – now the Luas Green Line – it has been the subject of a few "Save Airfield" campaigns even in the years since. But the 38-acre farm has survived. After a multimillion-euro revamp in 2014, its future looks secure.

The farm still has Jersey cows. It still has the Rolls Royce too, now almost as old as the sisters were, but in perfect working order. Not much else is unchanged since the 1920s. In fact Dundrum is synonymous these days with a huge, high-end shopping centre: a mecca for those in search of designer fashions and the like. In the meantime, just up the road, the cows still need to be milked daily, and Airfield Farm continues its mission to keep Dublin in touch with its roots.

Address Overend Avenue, Dundrum, Dublin 14, Tel +353.(0)1.9696666, www.airfield.ie | **Getting there** Bus routes 11, 14, 14c, 44, 44b, 75, or 116; or Luas Green Line to Balally | **Hours** Sep–May, daily 9.30am–5pm; June, Mon–Fri 9.30am–5pm, Sat & Sun 9.30am–7pm; July–Aug, daily 9.30am–7pm | **Tip** The milking of the Jersey cows is at 10.30am and 5.30pm daily.

2 _ The Anna Livia Fountain

A sculpture in internal exile

Her official name is Anna Livia, and she was supposed to be a poetic representation of the River Liffey, her long bronze hair merging with the fountain waters that once cascaded past her nude and elegantly reclining figure.

Alas, from the day she was first installed on Dublin's main thoroughfare, O'Connell Street, to mark the city's 1988 millennium, the sculpture was not treated with the dignity appropriate to a lady. Local scamps soon took to adding detergents and liquid soap to her bath to make it bubble. The less witty used it as a rubbish bin. Then there were the nicknames.

"Bidet Mulligan" (a reference to another Dublin folk figure, Biddy Mulligan) was an early leader in the field. The "Floozie in the Jacuzzi" was the one that stuck, in the process establishing a tradition whereby all new sculptures in the city were considered unfinished until they had a rude, rhyming nickname, like the "Prick with the Stick" or the "Tart with the Cart."

At the turn of the 21st century, after years of abuse, Anna Livia was finally removed to make way for work on another 1000-year monument: the Millennium Spire. She then spent years in dry dock somewhere, and was in danger of staying there. But in 2011, the city fathers restored her to public view, in more ways than one.

Shorn of her original granite surrounds, and now in pond water rather than a rushing fountain, she cuts a slightly sad figure in the Croppies Memorial Park, near Heuston Station. The pond water being shallow, she also looks a bit overexposed.

On the plus side, Anna is now at least closer to the river that inspired her. And when the park's gates are open – not as often as they should be – the more appreciative kind of passerby can escape the chaos of the nearby city quays for a while and join the much-maligned sculpture as she sits back and reflects upon the harshness of the world.

Address Croppies Memorial Park, Wolfe Tone Quay, Dublin 8 | Getting there Various bus routes, including 25 and 66, to nearby Parkgate St; or Luas Red Line to Heuston Station | Hours Varies with the seasons, but in summer, 10am–10pm | Tip Look for the plaque on the nearby Ashling Hotel (Parkgate St, Dublin 8), where the famous Viennese philosopher Ludwig Wittgenstein stayed during his time in Ireland.

3__ The Bernard Shaw Pub

A funky twist on a famous name

If you're looking for a good pizza in Dublin, and a fun place to eat it, you could hardly do better than the Big Blue Bus. An actual double-decker bus that once worked the streets of London, it is now permanently parked at the rear of the Bernard Shaw Pub on South Richmond Street. From this location, it sells freshly made gourmet pizzas to customers, who eat on board – in a miniature restaurant, with Moroccan-style decor – or in the bar's beer garden, where the pizza-on-wheels operation is anchored.

The bus is one of many things that set the Bernard Shaw apart – none of which have anything to do with its namesake. Yes, Shaw was born just a block away, on Synge Street. But literary tourists who turn up there looking for his birthplace museum, which is no longer open, and then think the pub might shed light on his life, will be in for a shock.

The Bernard Shaw doesn't look like the sort of place he would have frequented. It also – despite the "Established 1895" sign left over from a previous business – doesn't resemble any other Dublin Victorian pub. Instead, it's a funky, vibrant, young people's bar, set up in the early noughties by a "Dublin DJ collective."

The tone is set by the building's front, which was not so much decorated as attacked by graffiti artists. It continues with the music, which includes reggae, dub, house, "general electronic noodlings," and several other genres that, famous music critic that he also was, Shaw might struggle to recognise.

Then there's the drinks range, which would hardly have appealed to him either. He once described himself as "a beer teetotaller, but not a champagne teetotaller." And beer aside, in keeping with its disregard for Dublin pub convention, this is also one of the city's few bars where you can buy "Buckfast Tonic Wine": a brand better known elsewhere for being consumed out of brown paper bags in parks.

Address 11–12 South Richmond Street, Dublin 2, Tel +353.(0)85.1658406, www.bodytonicmusic.com/thebernardshaw | Getting there Various bus routes, including 14, 15, 15 a, 15 b, 44, 65, and 140 | Hours Bar: Mon–Fri 4pm–late, Sat & Sun 1pm–late. Big Blue Bus: Mon–Fri 5pm–midnight; Sat & Sun 1pm–midnight | Tip For a more genteel experience on the same street, at No 45, try organic tea and homemade cakes, perhaps while playing a game of chess, at Wall & Keogh's.

4_Bingo at the George
An old game with a new twist

A communal low-stakes version of the lottery, bingo retains a lingering popularity in Ireland, especially among women of a certain age. But the version played in the George bar every Sunday evening is not quite like any other.

The George is, among other things, Dublin's best-known gay pub. And its flamboyant bingo caller is the pig-tailed drag queen Shirley Temple Bar, aka Declan Buckley, a former Alternative Miss Ireland (1997). In her hands, the picking of the bingo balls is as much a cabaret act as a game. But it's a winning combination, clearly. After packing the crowds in for almost two decades now, it has become almost as much of an institution as the pub itself.

The George opened in 1985, a time when homosexual acts were still illegal in Ireland, and gay lifestyles had to be discreet or, preferably, invisible. The bar was a safe haven for people who might have suffered refusal of service, verbal abuse, or even violence elsewhere.

But in the intervening decades, a whole generation of Dubliners has grown up in an increasingly tolerant society. In 2015, as the George turned 30, it also enjoyed its finest hour, when Ireland became the first country anywhere to approve same-sex marriage by popular vote. The referendum result was announced in the courtyard of nearby Dublin Castle, from which cheering crowds spilled out onto the streets for flag-waving celebrations reminiscent of the World Cup homecomings of Irish football teams.

Gay venues are not nearly as rare in Ireland now as they were when the George entered the scene. In fact, a new wave of bars and clubs, including the Pantibar – fronted by another famous drag-artiste, Panti Bliss – may be cooler and edgier than the venerable establishment on South Great George's Street. But the George was out and proud long before it was popular. And in a milieu where royalty matters, it's still the queen.

Address South Great George's Street, Dublin 2, Tel +353.(0)1.4782983, www.thegeorge.ie | **Getting there** All City Centre bus routes | **Hours** Mon–Fri 2pm–2.30am, Sat 12.30pm–2.30am, Sun 12.30pm–1.30am. Admission is free Mon–Thu, and weekend nights before 10pm; after 10pm €5–€10 | **Tip** For a more conventional bingo game, head to the National Stadium on South Circular Road (www.nationalstadiumbingo.com), where thousands play every Tuesday, Thursday, and Sunday night.

5__Blessington Street Basin
A reservoir that turned into a park

When the Blessington Street Basin opened in 1808, it served a mainly functional purpose: as an urban reservoir holding 4 million gallons of water drawn via the Royal Canal from County Westmeath, to serve an ever thirstier city.

It did, however, also have a walkway around it, so the authorities made it available as a park for "well-conducted persons" in what was then an upmarket area.

But as the century progressed, other developments made the basin redundant, except to supply the whiskey distilleries. In the meantime, railways opened Dublin's seaside resorts to those in search of recreation. And by then the wealthier residents were migrating to the suburbs anyway, leaving the inner city to the poor.

So when the basin was first redeveloped as a park in the late 1800s, it was aimed at a different class of user: people with neither the time nor means to reach the city's bigger leisure areas – Phoenix Park and St Stephen's Green.

Another century later, the reservoir had entirely ceased to function, and was derelict. Then, in 1991, when Dublin was European City of Culture, an interesting possibility emerged. A famous German sculptor and "urban repair artist," Dieter Magnus, devised a plan to landscape it with ecological features, children's play areas, and more. Subject to local consultation, the German Cultural Institute agreed to fund the project.

But when residents were asked, they politely declined. The park had already been colonised by wildlife, they pointed out. It was already a local amenity. What they wanted was nothing elaborate, just an enhanced version of what was already there.

So in 1994, the basin reopened as a full-time park and bird sanctuary. It's a charming place, an oasis in an urban desert. But its charms are low-key and it doesn't advertise itself much. Which is why, more than two decades later, it's still a secret to most of Dublin.

Address Blessington Street, Dublin 7, Tel +353.(0)1.8300833, www.dublincity.ie | **Getting there** Bus routes 38, 38 a, 38 b, or 46 a | **Hours** Usually open from 9am. Closing times range with daylight hours, from 4.30pm in January to 9.30pm in June and July | **Tip** A narrow gateway at the eastern end of the basin leads to the Royal Canal Bank walk.

6_ Bog Bodies
Silent witnesses to an ancient past

He's known as Old Croghan Man, after the area where he was found in 2003. But he was probably only in his late 20s when he died more than 2000 years ago. And he must have been an extraordinarily fine physical specimen at that time, because what's left of him indicates that he was 1.91 metres (6.3 feet) tall: an impressive height even today, never mind in Bronze-Age Ireland.

His impeccably manicured fingernails and smooth hands tell us that he was of high social station too – perhaps even a king, or someone in line to become one. They also suggest he had recently enjoyed a meat-rich diet and so died early in the year, before his diet would have become more vegetable-based. But the contents of his stomach, preserved like the rest of his torso by Ireland's peat bogs, reveal that his last meal was wheat and buttermilk.

He died violently, from a stab wound to the chest, and after that he was decapitated. Gruesomely too: his nipples were cut off. One theory for this last indignity is that it marked his symbolic disqualification from kingship. In ancient Ireland, subjects demonstrated loyalty to a monarch by sucking his nipples, as a child does its mother.

In any case, his death was most likely a ritual sacrifice, perhaps in punishment for bad harvests (kings were always blamed for such things) and to help ensure better fortunes. His body was then staked down at the bottom of a pool close to a territorial boundary, sometime between the years 362 BC and 175 BC.

Today it's one of several such bodies displayed at the National Museum of Ireland. They include "Cloneycavan Man," of similar vintage, who retained his head and with it his crowning glory: a shock of long red hair. He too must have been a man of means, because although the rest of him is in bad shape, his hair is beautifully preserved, thanks in part to the expensive foreign gel he used on it, probably imported from France or Spain.

Address The National Museum, Kildare Street, Dublin 2, Tel +353.(0)1.6777444, www.museum.ie | Getting there Various bus routes, including 4, 7, 15 a, 15 b, 46 a, and 145; DART rail to Pearse station, then a 5-minute walk; or Luas Green Line to St Stephen's Green, then a 5-minute walk | Hours Tue–Sat 10am–5pm, Sun 2pm–5pm. Closed Mon. Admission free | Tip Nobel Prize-winning poet Seamus Heaney wrote *Bogland* about the extraordinary preserving properties of the peat bogs near where he grew up. He also wrote *Tollund Man* about the most famous bog body of all, found in Denmark in 1950.

7__Brendan Behan Sculpture
Monument to a writer and jailbird

In his later years, Brendan Behan used to joke that he was "a drinker with a writing problem." But long before he devoted his life to those twin activities, he was a self-styled freedom fighter, militantly opposed both to British rule in Northern Ireland and to what he saw as the sell-out Free State in the South.

As a 14-year-old he joined the youth wing of the Irish Republican Army. Two years later, he signed up for the IRA itself and embarked on a freelance mission to bomb the Liverpool docks, before he was arrested in 1940 and sentenced to three years in Borstal, Britain's juvenile prison system; an experience that would be the basis for his best-selling memoir, *Borstal Boy*.

Back in Ireland after his release, he was promptly rearrested for the attempted shooting of two detectives. Luckily for literature, he missed. Killing members of Ireland's Garda Síochána was a capital offence then and might have seen him hanged.

But his subsequent sentence in Mountjoy Jail inspired another work, a play called *The Quare Fella*, whose title character is a man awaiting execution. It was in this play that the ballad "The Auld Triangle" first appeared, describing the loneliness of prison life as regulated by the metal triangle rung to signal the daily routine, and echoing "all along the banks of the Royal Canal." The ballad has since been widely recorded by performers ranging from the Dubliners to Bob Dylan. And it's usually credited to Behan now, although he never claimed to have written it and almost certainly didn't.

At the height of his literary career, Behan was indeed as well known for drinking as for writing. But contrary to the joke, alcohol became the bigger problem eventually, causing the diabetes that killed him at 41, in 1964. Forty years later, his native city commissioned a life-sized sculpture of the writer sitting on a bench near Mountjoy: listening, not to the triangle, but to the song of a blackbird.

Address Royal Canal, near Binn's Bridge, Dorset Street Lower, Dublin 7 | Getting there Bus routes 1, 11, 13, 16, 40, 40b, 40d, 41, or 44 | Tip Among the best versions of "The Auld Triangle" are those by Luke Kelly and the Dubliners. You can find them on YouTube.

8_ The Brian Boru Harp

Possibly the world's most reproduced instrument

While the world beats a path to the nearby *Book of Kells*, another of Trinity College's treasures is often overlooked, although its symbolic importance to Ireland is arguably greater.

The Brian Boru harp is so named because it was once believed to have been owned by that High King of Ireland, who died in 1014. In fact, we now know, the instrument is not quite that ancient. It dates from the late 14th or early 15th century.

But that still makes it one of the oldest Gaelic harps in existence. And age aside, it may be the most famous, for two reasons. One is that it provided the model for Ireland's national symbol, ubiquitous on coins, stamps, and official stationery. The other is that, facing the opposite direction, it also became the logo of Guinness.

That Ireland is the only country in the world to have a musical instrument as its symbol hints not just at the importance of music throughout the country's history, but also the preeminence of the harp as a signifier of power and prestige. In Gaelic Ireland, skilled harpers had high social status. And when the old clan system was defeated, so were they. After the Battle of Kinsale in 1601, their semi-political role (and ability to double as espionage agents) led to an infamous order to "hang the harpers and burn their instruments."

But the most celebrated harp player and composer of all, Turlough O'Carolan, was yet to be born then, and the old-style instrument (wire-strung and played by the fingernails) was still popular into the 19th century.

As for the Brian Boru harp, though long silent, it made political headlines again in 1969 when a member of the Irish Republican Army stole it. Like most tourists, he had been more interested in the *Book of Kells*, but when he couldn't get that, took the instrument instead. He was later arrested while trying to collect a ransom, and the harp was returned unharmed.

Address The Long Room in the Old Library, Trinity College, College Green, Dublin 2, Tel +353.(0)1.8962320, www.tcd.ie/visitors | **Getting there** All City Centre bus routes; DART rail to Tara St or Pearse St, then a 5-minute walk; Luas Red Line to Abbey St, then a 5-minute walk; or Luas Green Line to St Stephen's Green, then a 5-minute walk | **Hours** May–Sep, Mon–Sat 9.30am–5pm, Sun 9.30am–4.30pm; Oct–Apr, Mon–Sat 9.30am–5pm, Sun noon–4.30pm | **Tip** Trinity College offers summertime accommodations to non-students. Visit website (see above) or call +353.(0)1.8961177.

9___Bull Island

An accidental gift to Dublin

Ten years after his difficulties with the mutiny on the *Bounty*, Captain William Bligh was given a less-exciting naval commission: to carry out a survey of Dublin Bay, which was notoriously prone to silting. In the process, he noticed the beginnings of an island caused by an earlier attempt to solve the problem: the "South Bull" wall. He also prescribed a new wall, on the north of the bay, which, when finally constructed in 1823, encouraged the embryonic island's growth.

Nearly two centuries later, Bull Island is now five kilometres long and 800 metres wide. It has one of Dublin's finest beaches on its seaward side, a salt marsh and wildlife sanctuary on the leeward, and two golf courses in between.

Uniquely for a site so close to a capital city, the island is a designated UNESCO biosphere. And as well as being a haven for many plants and animals, including orchids and migrating Brent geese from Canada, it attracts all human life too.

During the First World War, it was commandeered by the British army for use in trench-warfare practice. Since then, returned to civilian use, it has become a recreational treasure. Golfers aside, the island attracts walkers, swimmers, runners, triathletes, kite-surfers, and anglers. The flat, wide beach, with its compacted sand, is even popular with student drivers, who can access it via a bridge and causeway.

It also used to be home to a hare population, although that species seems to be in retreat now, even there. And it has been the subject of some hare-brained schemes too, including plans to turn it into a holiday camp and – much worse – a municipal dump. Mercifully, sanity prevailed. The island has instead continued to grow in useful-ness, just as it continues to grow physically. As for Captain Bligh's role, however incidental, it has turned into more of a bounty than his infamous ship ever was.

Address Clontarf, Dublin 3, www.northbullisland.com, www.clontarf.ie | Getting there Bus route 130 to Bull Wall; or DART rail to Raheny, then a 15-minute walk to the causeway | Tip The Bull Island Interpretive Centre is off the Causeway Road entrance (Mon–Thu 10.30am–4pm, closed for lunch 1pm–1.30pm, Fri 10.30am–1.30pm).

10__Bully's Acre
A cemetery with a lively past

Dublin's oldest cemetery, Bully's Acre has been a burial ground for at least a thousand years. But it was also once a notoriously lively place as well – too lively, often, for the liking of the authorities.

Both facts derived from its proximity to a holy well: St John's. This recommended it as a graveyard. But since the well was reputed to have miraculous powers, it was also popular among the living, especially on the saint's feast, June 24.

That of course coincided with mid-summer, the celebration of which predated Christianity. So festivities tended to combine "piety mixed with revelry and debauchery," much to the annoyance of the neighbouring Royal Hospital, a home for military pensioners, which tried and failed to close the cemetery down.

Even those interred in it were not always guaranteed rest. During the era of the "resurrectionists" – grave robbers who supplied bodies for dissection in medical schools – Bully's Acre was the scene of frenzied nocturnal activity. The trade was lucrative but had its risks. On one infamous occasion, a surgeon named Harkin and his accomplices were disturbed in the act. The accomplices fled, but Harkin – a portly man – was still clambering over a wall when caught. There followed a tug of war in which his friends tried to pull him over, while pursuers pulled him back. His injuries later killed him.

Of the hundreds of thousands buried in the cemetery, the vast majority are unknown. One very well known resident, by contrast, is the champion bare-knuckle boxer Dan Donnelly (1788 – 1820). But not quite all of him rests there.

Donnelly had an extraordinary physique, including freakishly long arms. This almost guaranteed his resurrection. And sure enough, the body was dug up. Then, after an outcry, it was reinterred, minus one arm which a surgeon had seen fit to keep, and which has been exhibited in various places ever since.

Address The Royal Hospital Kilmainham, South Circular Road entrance, Dublin 8 | **Getting there** Bus routes 13, 68 a, 69, or 79 a | **Hours** The gates to the cemetery are usually locked, but heritage tours are occasionally arranged through the Irish Museum of Modern Art (www.imma.ie) or military historian Paul O'Brien (www.paulobrienauthor.ie). | **Tip** Note the castellated rear entrance of the RHK near Bully's Acre. It used to be one of the gates into the walled city of Dublin but was moved to its current location in the 19th century after becoming an impediment to traffic.

11_Burdock's Chip Shop

Dublin's "oldest chipper," but is it the best?

Ask a crowd of Dubliners where the "best chipper" in the city is and you're guaranteed to start a lively argument. The question is as fiercely disputed as it is unanswerable. The fact that there's no official competition for the title doesn't deter people from wanting to award it.

Loyalty is an important factor. Many like to think their local chip shop is so obviously superior that there's no need to try any others. Nostalgia matters too. The chipper you used to eat in is often unsurpassable, especially if graduation, emigration, or a diet has since separated you from it forever.

The oldest surviving chip shop in Dublin, and a perennial nominee as the best, is Burdock's on Werburgh Street. A cartoon on one of its walls depicts a boatful of Vikings arriving in the city a thousand years ago and lining up outside the shop; a slight exaggeration, as it only opened in 1913.

But Burdock's *is* based in the heart of the old Viking city. And a mixture of location and reputation, now endlessly recycled by word of mouth, ensures that the still tiny premises are rarely without a queue. Also on the wall, a long list of former celebrity customers seems to include almost everyone of note who has ever visited the city.

Although chipped potatoes are a Belgian contribution to world cuisine, it was Italians who brought them to Dublin. It is also to Italians that the city owes its shorthand name for fish and chips – "one and one" – derived, apparently, from an immigrant who used the term *una di questa, uno di quella* ("one of this, one of the other") until it stuck. And Burdock's aside, Italian names still feature prominently in lists of contenders for best chipper. Lido's on Pearse Street, the Sorrento on Arbour Hill, and Aprile's of Stillorgan all have supporters. As does a Russian-owned chain, Beshoff's, especially for its shop on the harbour front in Howth.

Address Werburgh Street, Dublin 8, Tel +353.(0)1.4540306, www.leoburdock.com |
Getting there Bus routes 13, 27, 40, 56 a, 77 a, 123, or 150 | Hours Daily noon – midnight |
Tip On "National Fish and Chip Day" (usually late May), participating shops offer the
meal at half price.

12 __ Cavendish and Burke Cross

A dark episode in the life of Dublin's biggest park

The Phoenix Monument is not much to look at, really. But dating from 1747, it does at least have age on its side. It also marks the centre, more or less, of the 1752-acre Phoenix Park. And it serves as a pointer to the most notorious incident in the park's 300-year existence, which is otherwise very difficult to pinpoint.

It was about 500 metres south of the monument, one spring evening in 1882, that the British government's new chief secretary to Ireland, Lord Frederick Cavendish, and the permanent under-secretary, Thomas Henry Burke, were beset by a gang of knife-wielding assassins. Cavendish had arrived in Ireland only hours earlier. In fact, he was walking to the Chief Secretary's Lodge (now the U.S. ambassador's residence), where he was awaited, and had been joined en route by the Irishman Burke. The latter – an unpopular figure – was the assassins' intended target. They probably didn't recognise Cavendish, and killed him only because he defended his companion.

The killers were a new group of militant nationalists, the Invincibles, and their actions created shockwaves in Britain. One of their leaders, James Carey, later turned Queen's evidence, condemning five of the men to be hanged. Carey then became the subject of a witness protection program. This was supposed to give him a false identity and a new life in Australia. Instead, on the first leg of his trip, to South Africa, he was recognised by a fellow passenger who shot him dead.

One of the main protagonists, the getaway driver James "Skin the Goat" Fitzharris, escaped with a prison sentence and survived to make an appearance 18 years later in James Joyce's *Ulysses*. But amid the many memorials in the Phoenix Park, only a small pebble-filled cross, cut into the grass opposite Áras an Uachtaráin without commentary, now marks the scene of the infamous murders.

Address Chesterfield Road, Phoenix Park, Dublin 8, Tel +353.(0)1.82058000, www.phoenixpark.ie | Getting there Various bus routes to Parkgate St, including 25, 25a, 25b, 26, 66, 66a, 66b, 67, and 69; or Luas Red Line to Heuston Station, then a 5-minute walk to the park entrance. The Cavendish and Burke Cross is about a 20-minute walk from the park gates, left of the main road; the Phoenix Monument is another 5 minutes' walk | Hours The park is always open | Tip For a full history of the events of May 1882, read Senan Molony's *The Phoenix Park Murders: Conspiracy, Betrayal & Retribution*.

13__Central Bank Plaza
A popular space under a controversial building

When architect Sam Stephenson unveiled his new Dame-Street headquarters for the Central Bank of Ireland in 1975, it proved deeply controversial. In a low-rise city, it was almost a skyscraper. With its brutalist style of architecture, the building not only overlooked the narrow streets of Temple Bar, it seemed to overwhelm them too.

The final silhouette was not decided for many years because the roof originally exceeded city planners' height restrictions. And even after a compromise was reached on that, many people continued to hate the overall structure. When Éamonn O'Doherty's *Crann an Óir* ("Tree of Gold") sculpture was added at street level to mark Dublin's year as European City of Culture, a letter to the *Irish Times* suggested that only explosives would improve the bank's appearance.

Meanwhile, despite all the attention devoted to the building's effect on the skyline, the space underneath was worming its way into the affections of the city's populace, especially the young. The Central Bank Plaza became a magnet for Dublin's teenage Goths and Emos. Skateboarders loved it too: so much so, the bank eventually had to add railings to block off the steps.

As Temple Bar evolved into a frenetic cultural and tourism quarter, the plaza became one of its main gateways. But it also provided a haven from the traffic of Dame Street, its tree a useful meeting place. In the wake of the banking crash, at the height of the global "Occupy" movement, the plaza was also for a while the home of Dublin's tented protest village.

In 2014, forty years after moving to Dame Street, the Central Bank announced plans to relocate to the docklands. A new use for Stephenson's skyscraper – now broadly popular – is as yet undecided. So is the fate of the golden tree. It's officially still the property of the bank. But given the sculpture's potential relocation costs, the plaza is expected to retain custody.

Address Dame Street, Dublin 2, www.centralbank.ie | Getting there Various bus routes, including 13, 16, 40, and 123; Luas Red Line to Jervis, then a 7-minute walk; or Luas Green Line to St Stephen's Green, then a 7-minute walk | Tip For more information about *Crann an Óir* visit www.publicart.ie.

14__ The Chapel Royal
Chronicle of a revolution foretold

Dublin Castle was for centuries the seat of British rule in Ireland, a rule that must never have seemed more secure than in 1814. So it's all the more remarkable that the castle's Chapel Royal, completed that year, should have predicted Irish independence, and with uncanny accuracy.

Among the many opulent details in its neo-Gothic interior are the coats of arms of every person who served as Lord Lieutenant, the English monarch's official representative in Ireland. The epic series begins with Norman Hugh de Lacy in 1172 and continues through the likes of Oliver Cromwell (1649) right up to Charles Whitworth, appointed the year before the chapel opened.

Thereafter, new coats of arms were added whenever a Lord Lieutenant took up office. And where the earlier ones had gone onto the chapel's wood panelling, the later ones went on the stained glass windows. But it must have been apparent as the 19th century gave way to the 20th that they were running out of room.

Sure enough, when Edmund Talbot, aka Viscount FitzAlan, was appointed in 1921, his family arms went on the only space left. Events outside the castle, meanwhile, confirmed that the writing was on the wall for the old regime.

Ireland's War of Independence was by then in its third year, and FitzAlan – the first Catholic appointment for centuries – was an attempt at appeasement. It didn't work. An Anglo-Irish peace treaty later that year established a Free State and abolished his position, so the problem of where to put his successor's arms never arose.

The Chapel Royal replaced an earlier chapel that, in another omen, had developed structural problems. It was too heavy for the soft earth here, where the river Poddle runs underground. So the apparent monumental solidity of the new building is an illusion. It had to be light, and the "stone" pillars are actually stuccowork around wooden frames, as your knuckles can confirm.

Address Lower Castle Yard, Dublin Castle, Dublin 2, Tel +353.(0)1.6458813, www.dublincastle.ie | **Getting there** Various bus routes, including 13, 27, 40, 49, 54 a, and 747 Airlink to Dame St; or 9, 14, 15, 15 a, 15 b, 16, 65, 65 b, and 83 to South Great George's St | **Hours** Mon–Sat 10am–4.45pm, Sun noon–4.45pm | **Tip** Look for the 100 carved stone heads on the church's exterior, including impressions of Jonathan Swift, Brian Boru, and St Patrick.

15_ The Chester Beatty Library
Ancient script that made a translator blush

It's not widely known – or the venue might have long queues outside – that the Chester Beatty Library contains 3000-year-old writings from Egypt, the sexual frankness of which embarrassed their 20th-century translator.

An employee of the British Museum, the man had been retained by Alfred Chester Beatty, the U.S. Orientalist and collector, as a specialist on Egyptian texts. And after persuading Beatty to buy a group of papyrus rolls that had just come on the market, and then translating them for a book, he felt the need to warn his client about part of the material: "It is unfortunate that the original story becomes very licentious at this point and I have felt it to be my scientific duty to translate the [text] as it stands. ... I need not say that the obscene passages were not of my seeking but imposed by the material."

The publishers were also worried, but consoled themselves that the volume, being both expensive and aimed at specialist scholars, "would not be within reach of the ordinary man."

Beatty was living in London at the time (the 1920s and '30s), but he grew disillusioned with Britain's post-war government. And after he became a citizen of Ireland in the 1950s, he left not just the Egyptian material, but also his extraordinary trove of books, manuscripts, art, and artefacts – mostly from Asia – to his adopted country.

The collection is now housed in a beautiful museum at the rear of Dublin Castle. Complete with a Middle Eastern-themed restaurant, the Silk Road Cafe, it has been a worthy winner of the European Museum of the Year award. Its specialist nature still deters some potential visitors, however. As perhaps does the fact that it is officially a "library," even though it also contains such things as a prize collection of carved Chinese snuff bottles. Visitor numbers might also be greater if rude ancient Egyptian script was more widely understood.

Address Dublin Castle, Dublin 2, Tel +353.(0)1.4070750, www.cbl.ie | Getting there Various bus routes, including 27, 56 a, 77 a, and 150 | Hours Mar–Oct, Mon–Fri 10am–5pm, Sat 11am–5pm, Sun 1pm–5pm; Nov–Feb, closed Mon | Tip Once you've seen the museum, check out the roof garden.

16__ The Church

A place of worship to Arthur Guinness

When Arthur Guinness was married at St Mary's Anglican Church in 1761, two years after founding the now famous brewery, he can hardly have imagined that his stout would one day be sold there. But when the church closed two centuries later, such was the strange fate that awaited it. The building first lay derelict for a number of years. Then it was deconsecrated and sold, with a 15-year embargo on certain uses deemed unsuitable for a one-time place of religion.

It spent some of this buffer period as a home decoration store. When the time elapsed, however, and developers were free to do what they wished with the premises, it was transformed into one of Dublin's most dramatic pubs, serving not just beer and stout, but a range of whiskeys and cocktails that might make the more pious former parishioners turn in their graves.

Fortunately, they're no longer in their graves. Or at least, as part of the deconsecration, those who were buried in the crypt were cremated and their remains relocated to the nearby St Michan's. Which is doubly fortunate, in fact, because the St Mary's Crypt is now a nightclub.

Built between 1700 and 1702, and designed by the same architect responsible for the Royal Hospital Kilmainham, this was the first galleried church in Dublin. Guinness aside, its celebrity parishioners included Jonathan Swift. John Wesley preached in it. And among babies baptised there were future playwrights Richard Brinsley Sheridan and Sean O'Casey, as well as the republican martyr Wolfe Tone.

Another visitor was George Frederick Handel, who, prior to the world premiere of his *Messiah* – across the Liffey, in Fishamble Street – practiced the piece on St Mary's magnificent organ. Designed by Renatus Harris, the organ is still there today. So are the old church's stained-glass windows, while a more recent addition – a bust of Mr Guinness – links the building's uses old and new.

Address Junction of Mary Street and Jervis Street, Dublin 1, Tel +353.0(1).8280102, www.thechurch.ie | Getting there All City Centre bus routes; or Luas Red Line to Jervis, then a 3-minute walk | Hours Mon–Thu 10.30am–11.30pm, Fri & Sat 10.30am–2.30pm, Sun 10.30am–11.30pm | Tip St Mary's old churchyard is now the nearby Wolfe Tone Square.

17__Civic Offices on Wood Quay

An epic clash between Dublin old and new

Behind the Dublin City Council offices on Wood Quay is a small park and amphitheatre, occasionally used for outdoor performances. It's a pleasant place to watch a play or concert. But it's also the perfect location to reflect on a drama that was acted out around this site over the last two decades of the 20th century.

The trouble began back in the 1950s, when the city decided that this was where its new civic offices would be built. Various schemes were suggested, before a public competition was held in 1968 and won by the enfant terrible of Irish modernist architecture, Sam Stephenson. Even by his own standards, the winning proposal was controversial: four monumental granite blocks, with minimal windows, descending in steps – like the basalt columns of the Giant's Causeway – towards the Liffey.

But even as preparations went ahead to construct it, excavations revealed that the site included remains of one of the most important Viking settlements of Europe, and a section of the old city walls to boot. There followed years of legal challenges and protests aimed at stopping the development. The city first pressed ahead, building the two biggest blocks, quickly dubbed the "bunkers" by unimpressed Dubliners. Then they lost their nerve, and abandoned the rest of the plan.

Instead, a decade later, there was another competition to finish the site. And among the achievements of the development's somewhat more popular second phase was to help obscure the first. Today, finds from the original excavation are preserved off-site in the National Museum, while a section of the city wall is on display in a conference centre just beside the park. Meanwhile, although the protest campaign was ultimately defeated, the name Wood Quay continues to reverberate in Ireland as a byword for development at the expense of heritage.

Address Civic Offices, Wood Quay, Dublin 2 | **Getting there** Various bus routes, including 37, 39, 39 a, 70, and 83; or Luas Red Line to Jervis, then a 5-minute walk | **Tip** Look for the pavement inserts on Wood Quay, Winetavern Street, Fishamble Street, and Christchurch Place, representing tools, jewellery, and other artefacts found during the excavations.

18__Clondalkin's Round Tower

Pieces of ancient Ireland in a modern suburb

In Ireland, the ancient and modern are often forced into very close coexistence. This is nowhere more true than Clondalkin, a busy west-city suburb where among the things you encounter while walking the footpaths is a 1200-year-old round tower.

Round towers are a form of architecture almost unique to Ireland (there are a couple in Scotland and one in the Isle of Man). The structures are usually associated with early-Christian monasteries, and it used to be thought they were designed as places of vertical refuge from marauding Norsemen.

It's known that the monastery of St Crónán (aka Mochua) at Clondalkin was indeed pillaged by Vikings, more than once. But since the doors of round towers were likely wooden, and vulnerable to fire, the protective powers of a chimney-like stone cylinder are more than dubious. The structures are now believed to have served at least partly as bell towers.

Of the 60-odd examples still standing in Ireland, Clondalkin's is the only one within the city of Dublin. Twenty-seven metres tall and only four metres wide, it's not among the biggest of the genre. But it's unusual in having an intact conical roof. And although the date of construction is unrecorded, the tower's style suggests it may be one of the earliest, possibly from the 8th century.

Even that is young, however, compared with another of Clondalkin's attractions: the 5th-century St Brigid's Holy Well on Boot Road. The structure around the well is much more modern than that and, unfortunately, latter-day road widening has altered the flow of the underground spring so that the well – once thought to have miraculous powers – no longer rises here. But the site was renovated in the 1990s, and as demonstrated by the many votive objects left there, including the multiple ribbons tied to an adjacent ash tree, the cult of St Brigid remains strong.

Address Tower Road, Clondalkin, Dublin 22, www.southdublinhistory.ie | Getting there Various bus routes to Clondalkin village, including 13, 51 d, and 69 | Tip The grounds of St John's Church, opposite the Round Tower, contain some ruins from the old monastery.

19___The Cobblestone

A magnet for musicians

The Cobblestone is a well-named pub. It looks out over Smithfield Square, which is paved by no fewer than 400,000 cobbles (or more strictly "setts," being of regular shape rather than rounded stone). We know this because, during refurbishment some years ago, they were all taken up and cleaned before being relaid.

But the pub in question is best known for its live music – which, contrary to what the name might suggest, is not of the rock variety. The Cobblestone is instead synonymous with Irish traditional music, typically involving flutes, fiddles, tin whistles, and uilleann pipes, and played by friends or strangers combining in that Celtic cultural phenomenon called the "session."

There's a backroom venue for formal concerts and other events. Most of the sessions, however, happen informally in the front of the bar itself. And even there, the performances are taken very seriously. Multiple signs remind drinkers within earshot that it's not intended as background noise. This is a "listening area," they're told. "Respect the musicians."

The respect stems in part from that fact that the Cobblestone's owners, the Mulligan family, are musicians themselves, and have been for at least five generations. Of the current stock, Néillidh Mulligan is one of Ireland's best-known uilleann pipers. And that most extraordinary of instruments is showcased on the first Tuesday of every month, when the pub hosts Na Píobairí Uilleann for a special session. But there's some kind of traditional music every day or night in the Cobblestone, which hosts classes as well.

In fact there's a weekly event, held in the backroom and aimed at improving musicians, known jokingly as the "Balaclavas Session." Participants don't have to wear actual balaclavas. It just means they receive guidance or tuition, in an unexposed space, designed to equip them with both the skill and the courage, eventually, to play in the bar.

Address 77 King Street North, Smithfield, Dublin 7, Tel +353.(0)1.8721799, www.cobblestonepub.ie | Getting there Bus routes 39 a or 83; or Luas Red Line to Smithfield | Hours Mon–Thu 4pm–11.30pm, Fri 4pm–12.30am, Sat 2pm–12.30am, Sun 2pm–11pm | Tip Most of the music played in the Cobblestone is instrumental, but on the first Sunday night of every month, it also hosts a singing club. The club is named after a famous old Dublin ballad about a prisoner awaiting execution: "The Night Before Larry Was Stretched."

20__Connolly Books & The New Theatre

A haven for radicals in touristy Temple Bar

Despite its sometimes uneasy mixture of culture and hedonism, Temple Bar is an undisputed triumph of capitalism, with its crowded streets full of bars, shops, and restaurants competing fiercely for the tourist dollar. But the area still has vestiges of an earlier, less commercial age, and the communist-run Connolly Books is one of them.

It takes its name from James Connolly, the socialist leader executed for his part in the 1916 Rising, which eventually led to an independent but not very socialist Ireland. And the fate of earlier left-wing bookstores in Dublin illustrates the struggles of radical politics generally in the years since. The first shop was set up in 1932, and quickly had to move following complaints by a nearby Franciscan friary. The second was besieged and then burned down after a sermon in the Catholic Pro-Cathedral on the dangers of socialism. The third, around the corner from the current shop, was attacked in the 1950s.

As for this one, the Irish Communist Party opened it in 1976, at a time when the area was run-down and part of it earmarked to become a city-centre bus garage. The shop has since survived both the rise of touristy Temple Bar and the fall of the Soviet Union, somehow still intact.

Since 1997, it has also been the home of the 66-seat New Theatre. They're run as separate businesses, although mutually sympathetic: the theatre less overtly political than the bookshop, dedicated to presenting neglected Irish plays or works by smaller companies that can't afford to perform anywhere else. Both were threatened a few years ago by structural damage caused, in part, by the River Poddle, which runs underneath Temple Bar. Then a left-wing builder helped fund the refurbishment. And today the river flows on underground, while the lefty bookshop and theatre do likewise at street level.

Address 43 East Essex Street, Temple Bar, Dublin 2, Tel +353.(0)1.6708707 (bookshop), +353.(0)1.6703361 (theatre), www.communistpartyofireland.ie, www.thenewtheatre.com | **Getting there** All City Centre bus routes; or Luas Red Line to Jervis, then a 5-minute walk | **Hours** Bookshop: Mon–Sat 9.30am–6pm; theatre show time is usually 7.30pm | **Tip** The building that houses the bookshop and theatre is among the oldest in Dublin, dating from 1691.

21__The Countess and Her Dog

A bite-sized story from Ireland's revolution

The Countess Markievicz statue on Townsend Street has had its critics. Some complain it plays down her military role during Ireland's fight for independence. Others think it's just a bit twee. A writer from the nearby *Irish Times* suggested it looked like "a giftshop item enlarged."

But it is at least unique among Dublin political statues in also including the subject's dog – in this case a cocker spaniel named Poppet. And as such, it makes an interesting companion piece to a famous exhibit in Ireland's National Museum.

Like the statue, the real-life Poppet divided opinion. Some of Markievicz's republican allies disliked the spaniel intensely. It's said, indeed, that when she wasn't looking, he was given the occasional kick. But the countess herself was endlessly indulgent, even when the dog was guilty of anti-revolutionary activity.

Just before the 1916 Rising, for example, Markievicz had the task of making a flag for rebel headquarters. Because the shops were closed for Easter, she had to improvise by using a green bedspread, stretching it on the floor of her drawing room and getting others to hold it taut while she cut the shape. In typical fashion, the operation was closely monitored by Poppet – who, witnesses recalled, "kept jumping up and down pulling at the material, until eventually he tore a piece out of the side." Markievicz carried on, painting the words "Irish Republic" on the flag in gold. Then she smuggled it into the Irish Citizen Army headquarters, from which it was taken to the GPO, to fly from the roof during the rebellion.

The flag, on display at the National Museum, is now a revered symbol of the Republic's foundation, albeit a damaged one. This can't all have been the work of Poppet. Half the 'c' in "Republic" is missing, presumably shot away. But if the witnesses are to be believed, what was finished by the guns was started by an unruly spaniel.

Address Townsend Street, just off Tara Street, Dublin 2 | **Getting there** All City Centre bus routes; or DART rail to Tara St, then a 2-minute walk | **Tip** Compare the Townsend-Street sculpture with the bust of Countess Markievicz in the centre of St Stephen's Green.

22__ The Croppies' Acre

Tragic past, troubled present

The "Croppies' Acre" is one of the most impressive green spaces in Dublin, for reasons both good and bad. It's the supposed resting place of hundreds of republican rebels executed during the 1798 rebellion of the United Irishmen, a movement inspired by the American and French revolutions. Hence the nickname "croppies": from the rebels' hairstyles, cropped in imitation of the French and in opposition to the wigs then fashionable among the aristocracy.

The exact location of the "acre" was long disputed, partly because of the secrecy of the burials on marsh ground near the military barracks where the prisoners were held, and partly because of the redirection of the Liffey in this area when the city quays were being extended. But documentary evidence eventually pointed to what had become an army playing field, between barracks and river. And in the 1990s, for the bicentenary, the field was redesigned as a national monument: a tribute to the martyrs of '98 and "an area of meditation, reflection, and peace."

Alas, it was not long open before it became an area of drinking and drug-taking as well. Instead of flowers, discarded syringes and broken bottles were the tributes more likely to be left to the patriot dead. So, citing "anti-social activity" and a responsibility for public safety, the authorities simply closed the park.

Today, it remains closed: a very visible public failure, located between the barracks – now part of the National Museum – and, across the river, the main gate of the Guinness Brewery. Intrepid tourists can still visit it; the low wall and locked gates would not deter the athletic, just as they don't deter those whose activities forced its closure.

But it's worth your while walking around the park's outer perimeter, at least, for a short lesson both about Ireland's tragic past, and some of the harsher facts of its present.

Address Benburb Street, Dublin 7 | **Getting there** Bus routes 37, 38, or 39; or Luas Red Line to Museum | **Hours** Not open to the public; viewable from the outside | **Tip** For some of the history of Croppies' Acre, and the campaign to reopen it, visit www.theunitedirishman.blogspot.ie.

23___Daniel O'Connell's Bullet Holes

Hit in the crossfire of the fight for independence

It's the fondly held belief of many Dubliners that the front of the General Post Office is peppered with bullet holes. It was, after all, rebel headquarters during the 1916 Rising, when it came under heavy attack from the British army. And how else to explain those small round holes in the pillars and elsewhere?

So eyebrows were raised some years ago when, asked if renovations of the building would preserve these souvenirs of war, a GPO spokeswoman said the holes had not been caused by bullets at all. Amid resultant controversy, Dublin historian Pat Liddy leapt to the post office's defence, saying he had always been sceptical about the bullet theory, since the high-caliber rifles of British troops would more likely have caused splinter damage than neat round holes. Besides, the building had been largely destroyed by shelling and fire, and was rebuilt in the 1920s. As for the pockmarked pillars, to the chagrin of republican romanticists, those were probably the result of mere weather.

Where there undoubtedly are bullet holes from that period, however, is on the nearby monument to Daniel O'Connell. Erected in 1882, in honour of "The Liberator," it was very much in the line of fire during the fighting. The larger-than-life bronze version of O'Connell was hit repeatedly. Also injured were three of the four angels, each representing one of O'Connell's virtues, who guard the monument's base. The figure of "Courage" was shot through her right breast. "Eloquence" was hit in the elbow. In all, 30 bullet holes have been found throughout the monument, 10 of them on O'Connell himself.

It's an unfortunate fate for the statue of a great parliamentarian who abhorred violence. That said, arguably, none of the war damage is as detrimental to his dignity as the insults daily heaped on his head by pigeons.

Address O'Connell Street, Dublin 1 | Getting there All City Centre bus routes; or Luas Red Line to Abbey St, then a 2-minute walk | Tip Although famous for his espousal of non-violent protest, Daniel O'Connell once killed a political rival in a duel. When attending mass thereafter, he wore a black glove on the hand that had pulled the trigger, lest the sight of it offend God.

24_ The DART

A scenic rail route with its own accent

For most passengers, the DART is just a way to get in and out of Dublin from their homes in the suburbs. But it's also a great way to see the city, or at least the coastal parts of it, which are among the most attractive. The line connects the two "heads" that define Dublin: Howth in the north and Bray (actually part of County Wicklow) in the south, both popular seaside resorts. In between, it curves around the horseshoe-shaped bay, offering pleasant views and plenty of places worth getting off to explore.

For a mixture of geographical and demographical reasons, the DART hugs the coastline closer on the southern half. North of the city centre it cuts inland through Clontarf, Raheny, and Kilbarrack before hitting shoreline again at Sutton on the final leg of its journey.

But a thing you may notice if you make the full semi-circle is that the line undermines the popular concept that Dublin is divided between a well-heeled Southside and a poorer Northside. There is some truth in that, yes. As in most cities, though, if you live near the coast here, you're probably not poor. There are as many leafy suburbs on the DART's northern stretch as on the southern.

In fact, one of the criticisms of the service when it first opened in the 1980s was that it was an expensive subsidy of the middle classes. Generally, it was predicted to be a white elephant that would never pay its way. But the critics were wrong: it does.

A more bizarre criticism of the line was the supposed influence it had on the accents of people who lived nearby. Social commentators were soon identifying a self-consciously posh "Dart accent" (or "Dort" as the speakers were more likely to pronounce it) among the fashionable suburbanites who used it.

But it would be unfair to blame the phenomenon on a railway line. And besides, the Dart accent has since been heard in places as far away as the Irish midlands.

Address The main DART line runs between Howth and Bray, with extensions to Malahide and Greystones, Tel +353.(0)1.7033504, www.irishrail.ie | **Getting there** The main city centre stations are Connolly on Amiens St, on the Northside, and Tara St and Pearse Station, on the Southside | **Tip** If you want to explore Dublin's coast by DART, getting on and off at will, buy an adult day ticket for €11.10.

25 _ Door of Reconciliation
Taking a chance for peace

Among the many historic artefacts in St Patrick's Cathedral is a door with a very interesting rectangular-shaped aperture in it. You will hear in Dublin that the opening in question is where the popular Irish and British phrase "to chance your arm" originated. Unfortunately, it's not true. But it should be.

The Door of Reconciliation, as it became known, owes its fame to an incident in 1492, before which it didn't have a hole in it and was minding its own business in a doorway of the cathedral's Chapter House. Then a fresh dispute arose between two of Ireland's noble families, the Fitzgeralds of Kildare and the Butlers of Ormond, who were frequently at odds. Attempts were being made to resolve their differences over talks in Dublin. But instead the row escalated dangerously, with a member of the Butlers – Black James – and his troops forced to flee into the sanctuary of the Chapter House, pursued by soldiers with longbows. As a measure of how heated the chase was, it's said that many of the cathedral's statues were later found to have arrows stuck in them.

During the subsequent standoff, Black James refused the entreaties of the Earl of Kildare to come out and talk to him. So the Earl ordered his soldiers to cut the rectangular aperture in the door. Then, at the risk of losing his arm to an enemy axe, he thrust it through the hole to shake hands with Butler, opening the way for a peace deal and sealing the door's reputation for diplomacy.

The problem for etymologists is that the phrase to "chance your arm" didn't appear in print anywhere for another four centuries. One theory suggests it came from the more prosaic world of tailoring. Another says it derives from the risk involved in clearing the barrel of a jammed cannon. But Dubliners prefer their version. And whether it launched a phrase or not, the storied door is one of St Patrick's more popular exhibits.

Address St Patrick's Cathedral, St Patrick's Close, Dublin 8, Tel +353.(0)1.4539472, www.stpatrickscathedral.ie | **Getting there** Bus routes 27, 49, 54 a, 56 a, 77 a, 150, or 151; Luas Green Line to St Stephen's Green, then a 5-minute walk; or Red Line to Four Courts, then a 10-minute walk | **Hours** Mar–Oct, Mon–Fri 9.30am–5pm, Sat 9am–6pm, Sun 9am–10.30am, 12.30pm–2.30pm, and 4.30pm–6pm; Nov–Feb, same except Sat 9am–5pm, Sun 9am–10.30am, and 12.30pm–2.30pm | **Tip** St Patrick's is unique in having a choir school that dates all the way back to 1432. You can hear the choir perform daily during school terms. Visit St Patrick's website (see above) for details.

26___Dubh Linn Garden

A semi-secret garden best seen from the air

The way to enter Dubh Linn Garden, ideally, is by air. This is not as fanciful as it sounds, because before it became a landscaped park, it was a helicopter landing pad. And that function was preserved in the 1990s redesign.

Hence the circles of lights in the middle, designed not just to accommodate one incoming chopper but two (in the event that the passengers include a VIP, so that a decoy is needed). And even though the garden's maze of narrow paving strips – a Celtic design of two interlocking snakes – is purely decorative, that too is best appreciated from above.

But most people enter at ground level, via one of several entrances in Dublin Castle, and the garden is enjoyable from this vantage point too. In fact, if you have young children, you will find that the snakes have a mesmeric effect on them. No child can resist the urge to run around on the paved sections, which may have been part of a cunning plan by the landscapers to preserve the grass.

Although located in the very centre of Dublin (beside the site of the black pool, or Dubh Linn, that gave the city its name), the garden is either unknown to or forgotten by most city residents, so it's always a relaxing escape from the chaos of the streets outside, or even from the crowds of tourists in the main castle buildings.

It is, however, linked to the castle via a footbridge and tearooms. It also has the magnificent Chester Beatty Library (see p. 38) and the castle's own Coach House (a conference and exhibition space) as neighbours. The Coach House, by the way, was built partly for the amusement of a visiting Queen Victoria and partly to block from her view the backs of houses nearby. But newer, higher buildings have since joined the skyline to the castle's south. So now the castellated Coach House is just one part of a riot of different architectural styles onto which the garden looks.

Address Entrances off Dame Street, Castle Street, and Ship Street, Dublin 2, Tel +353.(0)1.6458813, www.dublincastle.ie | **Getting there** Various bus routes, including 13, 27, 40, 49, 54 a, and 747 Airlink to Dame St; or 9, 14, 15, 15 a, 15 b, 16, 65, and 122 to George's St | **Hours** Mon – Sat 9.45am – 4.45pm, Sun (and bank holidays) noon – 4.45pm | **Tip** As well as the Dubh Linn Castle Tea Rooms, the garden is also overlooked by the Silk Road Cafe, a Middle-Eastern themed restaurant in the Chester Beatty Library (see p. 38).

27__ The Dublin Canals

Royal, Grand, and lovely

Dublin is, among many other things, a city of two canals. These days they serve mainly as scenery, and as informal boundaries dividing the city centre from the suburbs. But they were built as business propositions, to link the city with the River Shannon, in the days before railways or reliable roads.

The Grand Canal is the older and the more successful. Finished in 1804, it curves around the southern half of the city before straightening out for the rest of its 132-kilometre journey towards the midlands. It was still used for its original purpose until 1960, when the last working cargo barge – carrying kegs of Guinness – left Dublin.

Younger and longer, the Royal Canal was completed in 1817 by a disgruntled ex-director of the company that ran the Grand. The newer waterway follows a complementary arc around Dublin's Northside and stretches for 145 kilometres. But it never really worked, and within 30 years the trains and roads that followed its path were sounding its death knell.

By the late 20th century, the Royal was barely navigable, but both canals are now having second lives, albeit with more action off the water than on. The towpaths, once the preserve of barge-pulling horses, are today being reclaimed by walkers and cyclists.

The Grand Canal also explains a joke that may mystify visitors to Dublin. It used to have a spur line to service Guinness' Brewery, passing under a bridge at the South Circular Road. When the bridge was rebuilt in the 1800s, although it was a functional structure with none of the romance of the one over the Grand Canal in Venice, wags took to calling it the "Rialto."

Not only did the name stick, it gradually extended to the surrounding area. Dublin thus acquired a suburb called Rialto. But then the spur line was closed and drained. So the Dublin Rialto Bridge now has no canal, grand or otherwise, under it – only the Luas tram line.

Address The Waterways Ireland Visitors Centre, which includes information on the canals, is at Grand Canal Quay, Dublin 2, www.waterwaysirelandvisitorcentre.org, Tel +353.(0)1.6777510 | Getting there DART rail to Grand Canal Station; or bus routes 1, 2, 3, 56a, or 77a | Hours Wed–Sun 10am–6pm, Mon & Tue by appointment only | Tip The centre also offers walking tours (Wed–Sat 11.30am & 2.30pm) of the adjoining area, telling the story of both canals and of "the race to reach the Shannon."

28 __ Dublin Doors
Poster-perfect entrances to a Georgian world

In the early 1700s, when Dublin acquired the Georgian doors for which it is now famous, they were all of similar colour. We don't know what that colour was, exactly, but it was probably something neutral and subdued, not the vibrant reds, blues, and yellows you see today.

A popular story is that the proliferation of contrasts began more than a century later with two literary neighbours who got on each other's nerves. George Moore, it's said, painted his door green to stop a drunken Oliver St John Gogarty mistaking it for his own at night. Then Gogarty painted his red to stop Moore doing likewise.

It's a good yarn, even if it isn't true. Whatever about Gogarty, Moore was not much of a drinker. In any case, it's likely that the owners of the city's Georgian houses had been expressing their individuality in door colours long before those two. After all, it was one of the few ways they could. Part of the elegance of Georgian architecture is its uniformity and perfect symmetry. Only in the trimmings – door colours, knockers, fanlights, etc. – could owners put their stamp on an exterior.

Dublin's Georgian inheritance went through a rough patch in the 1960s and '70s, when the poor condition of the older houses, combined with a tendency to modernise, led to the demolition of many. Their association with a hated colonial past, in an Ireland emerging from centuries of British rule, didn't help the cause.

It may have been a lucky break, when, in 1970, a New York advertising executive shooting a commercial in Ireland was struck by the beauty of the doorways and photographed 40 of them.

The resultant poster collage was used, first, for a campaign to promote Ireland in the U.S. Then the posters themselves became a commercial success, selling in the thousands, and demonstrating to anyone in Dublin who still missed the point that the classic doorway was one of the city's treasures.

Address Among the best places to see Georgian doorways are Merrion Square and Fitzwilliam Square, Dublin 2 | **Getting there** Various bus routes, including 4, 7, 25, 26, 44, 66, and 67 | **Tip** The Irish Georgian Society (www.igs.ie) organises walking tours of Dublin during the summer months.

29__The Dublin Port Diving Bell

A tiny museum telling an epic tale

A diving bell is not the kind of bell that rings, although for safety reasons, it might be fitted with a telephone. The "bell" part of the name came only from its shape. And rather than a clapper, traditionally, it had men inside, lowered to the ocean floor to carry out work.

The one in Dublin Port is a veteran of the epic construction job on the harbour's deep-water quays. It saw service from 1871 to 1958, and might have been scrapped thereafter. Instead, in the 1980s, it was hoisted onto one of the quays it had helped build – Sir John Rogerson's – and left there. For the next three decades, it stood as a tribute to the people who had turned the formerly tidal harbour into a deep-sea port. But it was a mute tribute. Despite the heroic story it had to tell, there was no plaque, or inscription, or anything else to explain this strange, red, weather-beaten object to the public.

Then in 2015, finally, the bell's silence was ended. By the simple means of raising it onto a platform, the structure was transformed into a miniature museum. Now you can walk in, read very informative panels about its history and, via watery sound effects, experience at least a little of the claustrophobia that the workers must have felt.

The bell, and indeed the quays, were the creations of a magnificently named Irish engineer, Bindon Blood Stoney, whose innovations included using massive concrete blocks – at 350 tonnes each, several times larger than any made before. These were lowered onto a seabed that had been flattened by the bell-workers. The men climbed down into the chamber via a funnel, and it can't have been comfortable working in the compressed air of a murky space smaller than most living rooms. But they and Stoney's design did the job. Despite the many risks involved, over nearly a century, the work never cost a life, or even a serious injury.

Address Sir John Rogerson's Quay, Dublin 2 | Getting there Luas Red Line to Mayor Square/NCI, then a 5-minute walk; or DART rail to Grand Canal Dock, then a 5-minute walk | Tip A brother of Bindon Blood Stoney was George Johnstone Stoney, the physicist who coined the term *electron*.

30___Dublin Snugs

Secretive drinking in pubs within pubs

A civil servant by day in the 1940s, the writer Flann O'Brien developed a habit of spending office hours in a local pub. On one occasion, a superior saw fit to give him a friendly warning: "You were seen going into the Scotch House." Whereupon, guessing that the informant had been drinking too, O'Brien shot back: "You mean I was seen *coming* into the Scotch House."

The need for discretion when visiting Dublin bars then was not confined to on-duty civil servants. Women, priests, policemen, and lovers often needed privacy while drinking. This might appear to be a contradiction in what were, by definition, "public houses." But the solution was the "snug," a discreet area sectioned off from the main bar.

The ideal snug had its own door, situated near the front or back entrance to the premises. It also had a hatch in the wall, with direct access to the bar. Windows, where necessary, had frosted glass.

Snugs could serve many purposes, privacy aside. If you were a writer, they could allow you simultaneously to eavesdrop on the main bar, without being taken hostage by pub bores (Flann O'Brien tuned his ear for Dublinese by listening to drinkers from a safe distance, although he was also a connoisseur of bores, "collecting" them for inclusion in his *Irish Times* newspaper column).

In some cases, they could be useful to the publican too, for segregating certain customers from the rest around closing time. The regulars could be ushered into the snug for after-hours service, while the main body of the house was cleared.

Today, the surviving snugs are mainly frequented by groups and for purely social reasons, not to hide away. The most popular ones in Dublin include Doheny and Nesbitt's, Kehoe's, and the Palace. But the issue of Ireland's best snug was put to a national vote some years ago, and that title too went to a bar in the capital: Toner's of Baggot Street (pictured).

Address Snugs can be found in bars throughout Dublin; Toner's Pub (pictured), 139 Lower Baggot Street, Dublin 2 | **Hours** For all Dublin pubs: Mon–Thu 10.30am–11.30pm, Fri & Sat 10.30am–12.30am, Sun 12.30pm–11pm | **Tip** Dublin snugs are usually available on a first-come first-serve basis, but pubs may let groups reserve them if asked nicely.

31 Dublin's Best Pint

A scientific approach to a long-debated question

The location of the "best pint in Dublin" is a question even more fiercely debated than the one about the best chipper. And it's almost as unanswerable. But there is at least some scientific guidance available to those in search of it.

By "best pint," it's understood that the drink is Guinness; all other pints are required to identify themselves by name. And it's a cherished belief among Irish people the world over that, unlike them, Guinness doesn't travel well. It's always of higher quality in Ireland, goes the theory, and even there, the closer to the brewery the better.

This might have been considered mere prejudice, but a 2011 survey by a heavyweight American publication, the *Chicago Journal of Food Science*, found some truth in it. Researchers studied pints in 73 pubs and 14 countries, using a ruler (to measure head depth), a stopwatch (for pouring time), and a checklist of various other quality indicators, while trying to rule out subjective factors, including the ambience of the bar. The results vindicated the prejudice: Irish pints scored an average 74 out of 100, compared with 57 overseas.

The researchers also considered explanations for the discrepancy, including what they called the "conspiracy theory." This is another popular belief, to the effect that the highest-quality Guinness is kept for the brewery's staff, the next best sold in Ireland, and the rest exported. But undermining this, the researchers found that the drinks served in the brewery were not the best they tasted.

They didn't go so far as to name the pub with the finest pint. They did, however, support the "line theory": that Guinness is best enjoyed in pubs where demand is high, so that it never sits in the pipes for long.

The advice to those in search of the best pint in Dublin, therefore, is to stay close to the brewery and look for pubs with a high Guinness turnover.

Address Look for a busy pub in the general vicinity of Guinness' Brewery, St James' Gate, Dublin 8 | **Hours** For all Dublin pubs: Mon–Thu 10.30am–11.30pm, Fri & Sat 10.30am–12.30am, Sun 12.30pm–11pm | **Tip** Regular contenders for the (non-existent) best pint in Dublin award include Ryan's (28 Parkgate St, Dublin 8), the Long Hall (51 South Great George's St, Dublin 2), Mulligan's (8 Poolbeg St, Dublin 2), Kehoe's (9 South Anne St, Dublin 2), Toner's (139 Baggot Street Lower, Dublin 2), and John Kavanagh's (aka the Gravediggers) at 1 Prospect Square, Dublin 9.

32_Dublin's Last Supper

An Irish twist on an Italian classic

Although it overlooks a courtyard in the so-called Italian quarter, Dublin's version of the *Last Supper* would hardly be mistaken for the more famous one in Milan.

It was created in 2004, at the height of the Celtic Tiger boom, a time of enormous change in the city. And to give a modern, Irish twist to da Vinci's masterpiece, artist John Byrne chose a cross-section of the real people who could be seen in the surrounding streets every day. About 150 were approached about taking part. After rehearsals and screen tests, they were reduced to a final 13 – three of them women – from a wide variety of social, professional, and ethnic backgrounds. The part of Jesus was played by an Indian Sikh PhD student. Bartholomew, by contrast, was a local tattoo artist.

Even the picture's backdrop is a cross-section. The main photograph (screen-printed in vitreous enamel on nine steel panels) was taken inside St Michael's and St John's Church, across the river in touristy Temple Bar. Another church, the ruined St Luke's in the Coombe, is also featured. The dome in the distance is on the Four Courts.

Like Jesus and the apostles, the supper itself is given a local flavour. Along with wine and fruit, the table has Irish soda bread and a teapot. Other curiosities include a Juventus football shirt draped over a chair: a nod to the Italian quarter's developer, a soccer-mad Italophile, Mick Wallace.

Ireland has seen even more dramatic changes since the mural's unveiling. After the banking crisis of 2008, Wallace was among many developers to experience severe financial difficulties. In the subsequent political turmoil, he won a seat in the Dáil (national parliament).

Despite some initial controversy, meanwhile, *The Last Supper* has survived to become one of the city's better-loved public works of art. And on days when the sun shines, at least, it provides the backdrop to Italian-style al fresco dining.

Address Bloom Lane, Dublin 1 | **Getting there** Luas Red Line to Jervis | **Hours** Always open | **Tip** For more informal street art, check out the car park of the Tivoli Theatre on Francis Street: site of the "Dublin Graffiti Hall of Fame."

33__The Ernest Walton Memorial

Reflecting two sides of a scientific genius

It's called *Apples and Atoms*. And given the location – the School of Physics – you'd be forgiven for thinking "apples" was a reference to the fruit that supposedly inspired Isaac Newton to a famous discovery in the 1600s. But on the contrary, the stack of silver spheres commemorates a 20th-century breakthrough that helped establish Albert Einstein's model of the universe at the expense of Newton's.

The man commemorated by it is Ernest Walton, an Irish physicist who with the English John Cockcroft first split the atom (or to be more correct, the nucleus of an atom). The 1932 event was the earliest practical demonstration of Einstein's equation linking energy and mass. And for good and bad, it marked the birth of the atomic age.

Both geniuses in their own right, Walton and Cockcroft met at Cambridge University and combined to form a perfect partnership. The Englishman was the theorist of the pair. The Irishman was the doer, who built the particle accelerator they used. Together, they won a Nobel Prize for their work.

Walton was only 29 when he had fame thrust upon him. He lived for more than 60 years afterwards, much of it back at Trinity College Dublin, where he had studied before going to England. In a country that has produced four Nobel-winning writers, he is still the only Irish person to get the prize for science. Yet colleagues recall him as a quiet, self-effacing individual. And he was as much at home in the garden as the laboratory.

Hence the memorial sculpture's title. As its creator, Eilís O'Connell, explained, the spheres represent Walton's highly ordered mind and a part of the famous accelerator. But the scientist also loved to plant fruit saplings, so the sculpture is flanked by two native apple trees. When you look in the mirrored spheres, you see their reflection.

Address The School of Physics, Trinity College, Dublin 2, Tel +353.0(1).8961000, www.tcd.ie/Physics | **Getting there** All City Centre bus routes; or DART rail to Pearse or Tara St, then a 5-minute walk | **Tip** While at Trinity College, visit the nearby Science Gallery, a free attraction with constantly changing exhibitions and a very fresh and innovative approach.

34 Francis Bacon's Studio

A workplace as a work of art

When the painter Francis Bacon died in 1992, he left behind an extraordinary collection of pictures, some of which now sell for tens of millions. But he also left behind one of the most chaotic artist's studios even seen. And when the Hugh Lane Gallery in Dublin – the city of Bacon's birth – decided that the painter's workplace was itself worthy of exhibition, it did something unprecedented in the history of art.

The studio had been presented as a gift to the gallery by Bacon's heir. But the first problem was that it was located in London, at 7 Reece Mews, Kensington. So before moving anything, the Hugh Lane first had to hire archaeologists to measure, photograph, and catalogue the studio's enormous amount of clutter: among it 2000 brushes and other artist's materials, 1500 photographs, 1300 torn-out book pages, and 100 slashed canvases.

They then tagged and packed everything, "including the dust." Even the walls, doors, floor, and ceiling of the studio were taken down. After that, the whole thing was shipped to Dublin and recreated, in every original detail, in a new, specially dedicated section of the gallery.

In the videos that accompany the installation, Bacon is seen explaining that the conditions of the studio were crucial to his work and that he couldn't have functioned in a tidy environment. Whether that's true or not, the art market has long ago decided that the end product justified the means.

Bacon's bleak, distorted paintings divided opinion in life, and still do. The former British prime minister Margaret Thatcher dismissed him as "the man who paints those dreadful pictures." Even one of Bacon's former lovers, whom he painted regularly, found the results "horrible." But when the paintings go on the market these days, very few buyers can afford them. One briefly held the world record for a work of art at auction, before being overtaken again by Picasso.

Address Hugh Lane Gallery, Parnell Square, Dublin 1, Tel +353.(0)1.2225564, www.hughlane.ie | Getting there Various bus routes to Parnell Square; or Luas Red Line to Abbey St, then an 8-minute walk | Hours Tue–Thu 10am–6pm, Fri & Sat 10am–5pm, Sun 11am–5pm | Tip Among the gallery's other treasures is Dublin's best collection of French Impressionists.

35__The Freemasons Hall

A secretive organisation now partially open to visitors

Ask most Dubliners what a Freemason is or does, and they'll tell you about men exchanging secret handshakes behind closed doors while working towards goals never revealed to non-members. Masonic lodges are indeed mysterious organisations. But anxious to counteract the notion of there being something sinister about what they do, Freemasons have been throwing their doors open to visitors in recent decades. In this practice, the hall on Dublin's Molesworth Street – headquarters for all of Ireland's lodges – has led the way.

The origins of the movement go back to medieval times, when guilds of actual stonemasons admitted certain pillars of society as honorary – or "free" – members. Since then, spokesmen say, the organisation has retained the trade's symbolism, while evolving into something broader, aimed only at the moral betterment of members and of society.

You don't have to be Christian to join; in fact, discussion of religion or politics inside the lodge is against the rules. Belief in a Supreme Being is enough, although in the higher ranks, where membership is by invitation only, Christianity is expected.

As for casual visitors to Molesworth Street, what they will see is a museum and the various rooms of a fine Victorian building, each replete with the movement's code of symbols.

A black-and-white chessboard carpet, for example, stands for the good and evil through which members walk in life. The opposed set square and compass signify the "square deal" they must offer others. The "all-seeing eye" represents the Supreme Being.

The policy of openness still has limits. The "means of recognition" remain a secret known only to members. And among the paraphernalia on display in the upper rooms are old-fashioned "ballot boxes," complete with funnels, drawers, and black and white beads. When a new member is under consideration, usually one black bead is enough for a veto.

Address 17 Molesworth Street, Dublin 2, Tel +353.(0)1.6761337, www.irish-freemasons.org | Getting there Various bus routes, including 7 b, 7 d, 11, 15 a, 15 b, 39 a, and 145; or Luas Green Line to St Stephen's Green, then a 10-minute walk | Hours In summer, Mon–Fri guided tours at 2.30pm. Outside these times, you may be able to arrange a tour by phone | Tip Despite certain similarities, the Freemasons have no connection with the Orange Order, an all-Protestant organisation, although the latter was founded in nearby Dawson Street.

36__Fusiliers Arch

A gate dividing two traditions of Irish history

For most Dubliners now, it's just the main entrance to St Stephen's Green, overlooking one of the busiest corners of the city, where shoppers, buskers, tourists in horse-drawn carriages, and the Luas Green Line terminus all converge. Nobody uses its official name – the Royal Fusiliers' Memorial Arch – anymore, even if they know it. And in fairness, not many use the scornful alternative title applied by some in the years after its construction: "Traitors' Gate."

Meanwhile, the memorial's original purpose is masked for most by the Latin of the inscription, which means in part: "Dublin dedicates this to her brave soldiers." As for the names of those soldiers, you have to look up while under the arch to see them: the 222 members of the Dublin Fusiliers who died fighting for the British army during the Second Boer War (1899–1902). By 1907, when the arch was built (modelled on the 1st-century Arch of Titus in Rome), sympathy with that war's losers and demands for Irish Home Rule made the memorial unpopular with many nationalists, who saw Boer generals like Christiaan de Wet as heroes and the Fusiliers as having fought for the wrong cause.

The classic Dublin ballad "Monto," written in the 1960s but set around 1900, sums up the case against them in typically irreverent terms: "You see the Dublin Fusiliers / the dirty old Bambooziliers / De Wet'll get the childer / One, two, three / Marching from the Linen Hall / There's one for every cannonball / And Vicky's going to send youse all / Over the sea."

"Vicky" was Queen Victoria, whose son would be the last English monarch to visit Dublin under British rule. Soon, like much of the city centre, the Fusiliers Arch was to suffer considerable damage in the fight for independence. But unlike many memorials associated with the old regime, it has survived into the 21st century, when the issues are no longer quite so controversial.

Address St Stephen's Green, Dublin 2 | Getting there All cross-city bus routes; or Luas Green Line to St Stephen's Green | Tip Just inside the Fusiliers Arch, representing the opposite tradition in early 20th-century Irish politics, is a monument to the Fenian leader Jeremiah O'Donovan Rossa.

1ST BATTALION
Cr Sergt V. J. Magee
Sergt J. Flynn
T. Callan
Corpl T. Lowe
J. Whylly
Lce Corpl P. O'Keefe
Pte A. Byrne
P. Usher
J. Toole
J. Cole
M. Nolan
J. O'Connell
M. Maddox
M. Hayes
P. Deery
Lce Corpl J. Wisdom
Pte J. Costello
J. Carroway
C. Joyce
J. Neill
S. Walsh
J. Donnelly
J. Young
Lce Corpl P. O'Reilly
Pte J. Landy
P. O'Raw
P. McKenna
A. Grierson
P. McCarthy
J. Walsh
W. Johnson
T. Reid
Cr Sergt A. Mulvaney
Pte P. Leary
L. Murphy
T. Moore

J. Scotcher
H. Scutcher
P. Monaghan
J. O'Keefe
H. Ellis
S. Smith
J. Robertson
Corpl T. Nesbitt
L. Conroy
Pte P. Brennan
L. Williams
J. Meehan
E. Gallacher
D. Moriarity
P. Dolan
J. McDonald
J. Byrne
J. Fitzpatrick
W. Murphy
Dr H. Allen
Pte W. Waddingham
T. Hanlon
J. Shields
J. Bell
C. Raynor
T. Eccles
P. Cullen
N. Lawless
J. Smith
P. McCormack
J. Mulligan
Sergt F. Price
Corpl J. Donohoe
Pte P. Lynch
M. Lee
J. Daly
F. Byrne
P. Byrne

2ND BATTALION
Capt C. A. Vernon
2nd Lieut J. Gemell
Pte J. Cahill
A. Merrill
J. Crotty
J. Callaghan
Cr Sergt F. Anderson
Pte M. Balfe
J. Birney
C. O'Shea
C. Johnston
Lieut R. C. B. Henry
Sergt E. P. Hayes
Pte J. Smith
J. F. Sinnott
J. Broderick
Lce Corpl W. Coyne
Pte F. J. Dillon
J. Murphy
J. Doolan
W. MacAlpine
E. Moore
P. Clifford
P. Flood
Lce Corpl J. Gibson
Pte J. Pearse
Lce Corpl J. Cathcart
Pte P. Murphy
A. Bennett
P. Campion
Cr Sergt J. Cage
Pte M. Phelan
O.M. Sergt W. Hynes

37__George's Street Arcade

A haven for Dublin bohemians

When the South City Market became Dublin's first shopping centre in 1881, the official opening was a decidedly elitist affair. The wealthy investors had employed English architects and builders to create the new venue ("brilliantly illuminated with the Electric Light" according to one newspaper advertisement). The natives were also snubbed at the gala luncheon, to their great resentment.

Nemesis arrived in 1892 in the form of a fire that destroyed most of the market. It had to be rebuilt, this time by indigenous craftsmen. And lessons were learned at the official reopening too, when all local representatives of any standing were invited. Since then, the George's Street Arcade – as it's better known – has established itself as a permanent fixture on Dublin's Southside, although its range of shops has changed dramatically over the decades.

Today the market is an eclectic collection of bohemian clothes and jewellery stalls, shops selling second-hand books and records, and cafés. There's also a fish-and-chips vender, a fortune-teller, and a couple of places devoted to "anatomical decoration." "Body piercing since 1973," proclaims a sign at one of the more time-honoured establishments.

Among other things, the arcade serves as a covered walkway linking the chaotically busy South Great George's Street with the quieter and more fashionable streets to its immediate east – a place with a village feel. Standing sentry at the George's Street entrance to the arcade is Simon's Place, a cafe where actors, students, and others on a budget enjoy soup and chunky sandwiches while watching the world pass.

The arcade also has a side door into the cavernous Market Bar, a former warehouse that retains its bare brick walls – one of them with a floor-to-ceiling display of shoe lasts – but is these days a popular pub and tapas restaurant, with its main entrance opening onto the neighbouring, ever more trendy Fade Street.

Address South Great George's Street, Dublin 2, Tel +353.(0)1.2836077, www.georgesstreetarcade.ie | Getting there Bus routes 9, 15, 16, 68 a, or 83; or Luas Green Line to St Stephen's Green, then a 10-minute walk | Hours Mon–Wed & Sat 9am–6.30pm, Thu 9am–8pm, Fri 9am–7pm, Sun 11am–6pm | Tip The wider south side of the arcade gets most of the pedestrian traffic. It's easy to miss the narrow north side, but there are shops there too, including a good second-hand bookstore.

38_ The Gravediggers Pub

A bar with a passing trade

Officially John Kavanagh's, the Gravediggers Pub earned its better-known nickname from the thirsty clientele who work next door in Glasnevin Cemetery. Not that the cemetery has a door. And there's no truth either to a myth that the pub used to have a special serving hatch through which pints of beer were passed directly into the graveyard.

It is true, however, that there was a system of knocks on the wall – sometimes involving shovels – to indicate when drinks were required. On that cue, pints were brought outside and handed through the railings.

Founded in 1833, a year after Glasnevin, Kavanagh's seems to have cornered its own piece of eternity. The pub has since passed through six generations of the same family, with the seventh and eighth now working behind the bar, but it can't have changed much in 180 years. There are still no televisions or piped music. A ring-board is the main entertainment. Although the usual other drinks are sold, this is the sort of place where most customers still drink Guinness, of which the Gravediggers is reputed to serve a particularly good pint.

Kavanagh's sole nod towards modernity was a decision, some time ago, to introduce a limited food menu, which involves lunch from Monday to Friday and evening tapas from Tuesday to Saturday, in the lounge.

Paradoxically, the pub's appearance has earned it a role in several movies. Such occasions aside, it remains a place to drink and talk, quietly, or at least not in a manner to disturb the "One Million Dubliners" (the name of a much-praised 2014 film documentary about Glasnevin) who rest in peace next door.

Kavanagh's, by the way, is said to have its own ghost. On his rare appearances, he sits in a corner, near the ring-board, wearing an old-fashioned waistcoat, wing collar, and pince-nez. Nobody knows who he is, although it's presumed his permanent address is on the other side of the railings.

Address 1 Prospect Square, Dublin 9, Tel +353.(0)1.8307978, Facebook: John Kavanagh "The Gravediggers" | Getting there Bus routes 13, 19, 19 a, 40 (a, b, c, d), or 83 | Hours Mon–Fri 10.30am–11.30pm, Sat 10.30am–midnight, Sun 12.30pm–11pm | Tip The Dublin Ghost Bus Tour, starting in the city centre, includes a trip to Kavanagh's (www.ghostbusdublin.com).

39_ The Great South Wall

A bracing walk into Dublin Bay

On a map of Dublin, the area around Ringsend Docks looks vaguely like a revolver, pointed in the general direction of Wales. It even has a trigger, on the south of the peninsula. And from the barrel of the gun, a thin line emerges, like the trace of a bullet, heading straight out to sea, before deflecting slightly and then hitting a lighthouse.

The thin line is the Great South Wall. And in reality, it's a lot more substantial than it looks on a map: being nine metres across at the top and wider at the base. Which is just as well, or the last section of its journey into Dublin Bay would feel even more exposed than it does. As it is, it's the most exhilarating walk or jog in the city.

The bad news is that, to get there, you have pass through some of the ugliest industrial landscape you'll ever see. The aforementioned revolver comprises reclaimed land and is used for such unglamorous purposes as the Dublin wastewater treatment plant, which is every bit as fragrant as you might fear. But if you're in a car, at least, you can pass it quickly.

Three centuries old now, the Great South Wall was an early attempt to prevent the silting to which Dublin Bay was prone. It eventually took the North Wall, built more than 100 years later, to solve the problem fully. But even if it wasn't a complete success, the South Bull Wall (as it's also known) was a major engineering achievement, being the world's longest sea wall at the time.

Much of the original structure is now part of the peninsula, and inaccessible to the public. But there's enough of the walkable section left to fill your lungs with fresh sea air and make the purgatorial trip through the wasteland worth it. And it's not all about exercise. Waiting for you at the end of the wall, as well as the Poolbeg Lighthouse, is a panorama of Dublin you won't see anywhere else.

Address Pigeon House Road, Ringsend, Dublin 4 | **Getting there** Bus route 18 to terminus at Sean Moore Rd, then a 20-minute walk | **Tip** En route to the Great South Wall, look out for the twin Poolbeg Chimneys: once considered an eyesore, they're now increasingly regarded as important Dublin landmarks, worthy of protection.

40_Hamilton's Equation

One small scratch for man, one giant leap for mathematics

One day in October 1843, the mathematician William Rowan Hamilton was walking along the towpath of Dublin's Royal Canal when he had a brainwave about a problem that had long frustrated him. He later described the moment in a letter to a friend: "… An electric circuit seemed to close, and a spark flashed forth."

He had discovered a formula for calculating quaternions, a way of extending complex numbers into higher spatial dimensions. And so excited was he by the breakthrough that right there and then he scratched the equation ($i2 = j2 = k2 = ijk = -1$) into the stone of the nearby Broom Bridge with his penknife.

His small act of vandalism has long since vanished. In fact, it had disappeared by the time a young math student named Eamon De Valera went looking for it half a century later. But the same De Valera went on to become Taoiseach (Irish prime minster). And as such, in 1958, he unveiled a stone plaque on the bridge that now records Hamilton's "flash of genius" more indelibly.

Quaternions were and remain so complicated that their inventor wrote several books trying to explain them, the last one stretching to 800 pages. In fact, after he died, this type of calculation went out of fashion for a while, replaced in science and engineering by vector notation. But it's a measure of how far ahead of his time he was that Hamilton's quaternions made a comeback in the late 20th century, being used in such things as computer graphics and orbital mechanics. When a spacecraft is sent to the moon or Mars, quaternions are crucial to its getting there.

Back on Earth, meanwhile, the original stroke of genius is commemorated annually on its anniversary, October 16, by the Hamilton Walk, which retraces the mathematician's steps from Dunsink Observatory (where he worked) to Broom Bridge.

Here as he walked by
on the 16th of October 1843
Sir William Rowan Hamilton
in a flash of genius discovered
the fundamental formula for
quaternion multiplication
$i^2 = j^2 = k^2 = ijk = -1$
& cut it on a stone of this bridge

Address Broom Bridge, Cabra, Dublin 7 | Getting there Commuter trains run between Connolly Station and Broombridge Station; or bus route 120 | Tip Dunsink Observatory (www.dias.ie) holds free open nights on the first and third Wednesdays of the winter months (October to March).

41__ The Hellfire Club

A beauty spot with a sinister history

The views from Montpelier Hill are among the most spectacular anywhere around Dublin. On a clear day, you can see the whole city and, far beyond it, the Cooley and Mourne Mountains, 100 kilometres away to the north.

But it's the murkier associations of the hill, and the oddly shaped ruin on top of it, that attract many people to these parts. Montpelier House was built in 1725 as a hunting lodge for William Conolly, one of Ireland's richest men. And even from the start, according to local tradition, it was ill-omened. The builders had used material from a nearby cairn – an ancient burial mound. So it was no surprise to some when the slate roof was promptly blown off the new house by a storm, forcing the owner to reroof it with stone, which remains intact today.

But the building's real notoriety dates from the late 1730s, after Conolly's death, when it became a regular meeting place for the so-called "Hellfire Club": an association of idly rich young men who delighted in scandalising society. No authoritative accounts of their activities exist. They were reputed, however, to involve everything from feats of epic drinking (especially of a concoction called "scaltheen": a hot brothlike mixture of whiskey, butter, and other ingredients) to Satanism. On at least one occasion, it was said, they soaked a black cat in the scaltheen and set fire to it as a sacrifice.

Worse than that, however, was the drunken row in which a leading club member, Richard Chappell Whaley, doused one of his servants in alcohol and set him alight. In trying to save himself, the unfortunate victim spread the fire to the house, burning several club members to death.

After that, the club moved to another local building, the Stewards House, which still stands. And up until recent times, at least, it was claimed by some visitors to be haunted by a giant red-eyed black cat.

Address Kilakee, Rathfarnham, County Dublin | Getting there The nearest bus route is 15 b to Stocking Lane, then a long walk; if driving, there's a car park for the Hellfire Club on the R 115 between Rathfarnham and Glencullen | Tip While in the area, you should also visit the former Massy Estate, now laid out as a forest walk with sights including a Bronze Age wedge tomb.

42_Henrietta Street

A riches-to-rags story

A cul-de-sac of fewer than 20 large houses, Henrietta Street has been part of Dublin for almost 300 years, and in that period could be said to have had three very different lives. It started out in the 1720s as an enclave of homes for the city's super-rich, with grand staircases, ballrooms, and all the other facilities their lavish lifestyles required.

Then, in the 19th century, the wealthy departed for the newly fashionable suburbs, at which point the street began a long descent to the other end of the property market. The giant houses became tenements for Dublin's poor, with whole families living in single rooms and staircases ripped out to fit more people in.

Finally, in the later decades of the 20th century, the residents of the tenements were rehoused and Henrietta Street embarked on its third, and least certain, phase of existence – its architectural importance as a crumbling jewel of Georgian Dublin universally recognised, but the money and will to save it hard to find.

Today, many of the buildings continue to deteriorate, but some have been luckier than others. Nos 15 and 16 are now the well-funded headquarters of Na Píobairí Uilleann, the Irish pipers society, itself a great success story of recovery from the brink of extinction. No 14 is being developed as a museum of the Dublin tenement experience, a fitting role for a house that in the middle of the last century was home to 100 people belonging to 17 different families.

And then there's No 12, which has been semi-restored and can be booked for arts-related events deemed appropriate to its condition. These range from intimate readings to eccentrically themed dinners and parties. But like the street itself, the interior of No 12 is especially popular with filmmakers. More than 40 movies have had scenes shot there at one time or another, taking advantage of the backdrop of distressed but still awe-inspiring grandeur.

Address Henrietta Street, Dublin 1, www.pipers.ie (for Nos 15 and 16, Na Píobairí Uilleann), www.dublintenementexperience.com (for No 14, the Dublin Tenement Experience) | Getting there Various bus routes, including 1, 11, 16, and 46 a | Hours No 12: Open by appointment for arts and cultural events (Tel +353.(0)1.8734964) | Tip If you're passing by No 12, you could try knocking on the door. Somebody might just let you in and show you around.

43__The "Home" Memorial
A monument to the victims of drugs

One of Dublin's sadder sculptures is located in middle of a road junction between Buckingham Street and Sean MacDermott Street in the north inner city. It's called simply *Home*, and it features a gilded bronze torch in a kind of doorway made from limestone. But the story behind it, and indeed in it, is one of loss and pain.

Before the monument was created, locals in this impoverished area had taken to erecting a Christmas tree on the spot every year, decorated with a silver star for each young person from the community who had died, directly or otherwise, from heroin use.

By the year 2000, there were 124 stars on the tree. But although it was a touching memorial, it was also a temporary one, and families were disappointed to see it taken away each year. So it was decided to erect a permanent memorial at the site, and public funding was made available.

Although artists were involved in planning the project, the selection process was unusually democratic. The winning design, from a short list of six, was chosen by a panel not of art experts but of people who had been bereaved by drugs.

The families had an even more personal input too. Before the chosen artist, Leo Higgins, cast the bronze for the sculpture, relatives were invited to bring mementoes of their loved ones to add to the molten metal. This revived an old tradition of church-bell making, whereby a congregation would bring keepsakes to add to the mix, so that the bell's ringing would have personal resonance. In the case of the sculpture, families added their children's Holy Communion medals, toys, and photographs to the flame.

The memorial was then deliberately located in a very prominent place, even at the expense of having to redirect traffic, as a signal to the local drug dealers, and to those in authority who had tolerated the heroin epidemic in a poor community for far too long.

Address Junction of Buckingham Street and Sean MacDermott Street, Dublin 1,
Tel +353.(0)1.8556735, www.firestation.ie | **Getting there** All O'Connell St bus routes; or
DART rail to Connolly Station, then a 5-minute walk | **Tip** Close to where the sculpture is
located, look out for the ivy-clad Aldborough House on Killarney Street, built in the 1790s
and once one of the finest residences in Dublin, but now unoccupied and derelict.

44 __ The House of the Dead

Home to the most famous dinner party in literature

Despite its name, the "House of the Dead" – aka No 15 Usher's Island – is more of a tribute to living than dying. It's yet another Dublin address associated with James Joyce. Two of his real-life aunts ran a music school there and hosted a late Christmas dinner for their students and friends every January 6: the Feast of the Epiphany.

So when Joyce made it the setting for his (very long) short story *The Dead*, he was paying tribute to his aunts' parties in particular and, in general, to the tradition of hospitality he considered central to the Irish way of life.

The guests in the story eat, drink, and take turns singing or playing piano. But what gives *The Dead* its title is the way departed friends dominate the conversation and music, especially one song, "The Lass of Aughrim," which inspires a personal epiphany for the lead character and the story's famously elegiac ending.

The narrative took on added poignancy when, in 1987, Hollywood director John Huston made a movie version. He was himself dying at the time and directed the film from a wheelchair. A full-scale model of the interior of No 15 was re-created for the purpose in a studio in Los Angeles.

Usher's Island is no longer an island, by the way. It used to be one, in the middle of the Liffey. Now it's attached to a stretch of the Liffey quays, although it's said that a former Dublin correspondent of a British media organisation used to delight in claiming for ferry trips to and from it as part of his expenses.

The real house was saved from dereliction some years ago by lawyer and Joycean Brendan Kilty, who now re-creates the "Dead Dinner" on January 6 and other occasions. The house also sometimes hosts exhibitions, and has a coffin in the basement left over from one such event. But like the story, the events in No 15 tend to be lively affairs, revolving around food, drink, and music.

Address 15 Usher's Island, Dublin 2, Tel +353.(0)86.0548880, www.jamesjoycehouse.ie |
Getting there Bus routes 25, 25 a, 25 b, 66, 66 a, 90, or 145; or Luas Red Line to
Museum, then a 5-minute walk | **Hours** By appointment | **Tip** As a tribute to the Joycean
connection, the bridge opposite No 15, by Santiago Calatrava, is designed to suggest an
opening book.

45_ The Hungry Tree
Nature's revenge on law libraries

The list of Ireland's "heritage trees" includes the ancient (an 800-year-old yew), the prodigious (a 40-metre-high ash), and the historically interesting (a copper beech signed by W B Yeats and George Bernard Shaw, among others).

The Hungry Tree in Dublin is none of these things. It's a London plane tree: mediocre in appearance, without famous autographs and, at 120 years old or so, of no great age. The only thing that sets it apart, in fact, is that for most of its life it has been gradually devouring a bench.

The wrought-iron bench was there first: it dates from the early 1800s. But current trends suggest that the tree will last longer. In the meantime, the disappearing piece of furniture is much photographed. You can still sit on it too, if you dare.

There may be an instructive metaphor here somewhere, because the Hungry Tree is located on the grounds of the King's Inns, Ireland's school for barristers, whose more venerable members tend to end up "on the bench" – i.e., become judges.

King's Inns was established in Dublin way back in 1541, under Henry VIII, making it even older than Trinity College. Construction of the current headquarters started in 1800, overseen by the great architect of Georgian Dublin, James Gandon, but finished by one of his pupils. Famous graduates of the body include Edward Carson, who led Ulster Unionist opposition to Home Rule for Ireland; and Padraig Pearse, who led the subsequent 1916 Rising, aimed at complete separation from Britain. Irish president Mary Robinson also studied there.

They, like all King's Inns students, benefitted from the school's outstanding library, built in 1832. The library now contains more than 110,000 volumes. And that may be one of the many possible explanations for the hungry tree's extraordinary behaviour: a small act of revenge for its countless comrades sacrificed to the insatiable needs of legal literature.

Address King's Inns, Constitution Hill, Dublin 7, Tel +353.(0)1.8744840, www.kingsinns.ie | **Getting there** Bus routes 4, 19, 19 a, 83, or 140 | **Hours** Daily, 7am–7.30pm | **Tip** Other heritage trees of Ireland are listed at www.treecouncil.ie.

46_ The Icon Walk

Reclaiming the back alleys of Temple Bar for art

Off the main drag in heavily touristed Temple Bar is a series of lanes and alleys that used to be unknown to visitors, and is still a fairly well kept secret. It was and remains a service area at the rear of business premises. But until recently the streets were dirty, and sometimes dangerous, being popular only with drug users. Culturally, in what was supposed to be the cultural quarter, it was dead space.

Then an artists collective called the Icon Factory decided to reclaim it for civilisation, colonising the walls with prints and paintings. The unifying theme was Irish cultural "icons": people who have done great things in music, literature, or sport. In part, it was a response to the economic crash that ended the Celtic Tiger years, when Ireland seemed to have gone from poverty to dazzling wealth within a decade.

The "Icon Walk," as the mural project became known, was a self-help initiative by artists who realised "we were on our own." And in expressing and developing their talents, they chose as their subject musicians, writers, and athletes: "the disparate elements which never disappointed us during The Great Delusion."

The street exhibits are half pictorial, half text, including biographical profiles of their subjects and the artists' mission statements, while taking time out for occasional frivolities, like the row of spiked metal security fencing now cleverly repainted to look like a set of colouring pencils.

Local businesses have chipped in with help and sponsorship. But the artists also contribute to a gallery-*cum*-shop at the centre of the walk: a nonprofit charity, proceeds from which fund the work.

The results have included a major increase in the footfall of pedestrians venturing off Fleet Street into the hitherto uncharted lanes. And as for the civilising effect, the artists claim that the incidence of crime in the area has already declined.

Address Aston Place, Dublin 2, Tel +353.(0)86.2024533, www.iconfactorydublin.ie | Getting there Various bus routes to Westmoreland St, including 1, 16, 25, 46 a, 67, and 118 | Hours Shop: Daily 11am–6pm. Exhibition: Always open | Tip For more street icons in this area, look for the four literary plaques on the footpath outside the Palace Bar (see p. 164).

47 The Irish Camino

Starting gate for an ancient pilgrim route

The Camino de Santiago, or "Way of St James" is one of the world's oldest pilgrimage routes. It still ends, as it always has, in Santiago de Compostela, Spain, supposed burial place of the apostle. But there were many different starting points, traditionally, and Dublin has one – in St James' Street, of course. As a sign on St James' Catholic Church confirms, "The Camino begins here."

People were heading for Spain from this area as far back as 1220, at least, which must have been around the pilgrimage's medieval peak, before the Black Death and the Reformation undermined it. And it's not that hard, even today, to imagine St James' Street as part of the narrow way along which penitent pilgrims went. Indeed, speaking of things black, the Dublin Camino now passes through an urban canyon formed by the buildings of Guinness, whose famously dark beer has been the indirect cause of many things for which Irish sinners have to atone.

Although the old St James' Gate, once the western entry into the city, no longer exists, there is a modern gate at the spot, on the side of the street, rather than across it. But penitents beware: it leads into the brewery, not to Spain.

That also explains the many "pilgrims" you may see here, passing in the opposite direction, towards the Guinness Storehouse, the city's most visited attraction.

In fact the influences of alcohol are everywhere in this area. It might have been a sobering thought for pilgrims of old that Dublin's two great medieval cathedrals, which you still pass on the route, are both now, in a way, monuments to drink. St Patrick's owed its 19th-century restoration to Benjamin Guinness, while the Christchurch job was paid for by a whiskey maker. As for the "other" St James' Church, the deconsecrated Anglican one: that is now being restored, but only as part of its transformation into a distillery.

THE
CAMINO
BEGINS
HERE

Santiago
CAMINO
SOCIETY.IE

Address Church of St James the Great, St James' Street, Dublin 8, Tel +353.(0)1.4531143, www.stjamesparish.ie | **Getting there** Bus routes 13, 40, or 123 | **Hours** Camino information centre: Thu–Sat 10.20am–3.30pm; Camino passports available from sacristy Mon–Fri 9am–noon | **Tip** Camino information and passports are also available from the Irish Society of the Friends of St James on Baggot Street (Tel +353.(0)85.7819088, www.caminosociety.ie).

48___ The Irish Jewish Museum
A tiny community that left a big mark

Some of the Jewish immigrants who came by boat to Dublin in the years before the First World War thought they had landed in America. By the time they found out, it was too late. So they took another boat trip, up the canal to Portobello, which in time became "Little Jerusalem," although there were only 5000 Jews there at most.

They could have come to worse places. It's not well remembered that Daniel O'Connell, "the Liberator," who brought Catholic emancipation to Britain and Ireland in 1829, had sought the same for Jews. And even today, according to one of their community leaders, Ireland is "the only country in Europe where not one Jewish person has been killed because of religious belief."

Tiny as the terraced houses of Portobello are, they were sometimes shared by two families. But the community thrived for several decades, becoming part of the fabric of the city. Then the younger generations began to emigrate. By the 21st century, there were fewer than 2000 Jews left, although a measure of their success was that, for a time in the 1990s, there were three Jewish members in the 166-strong Dáil (Irish parliament).

The Irish-Jewish museum is based in a pair of terraced houses, including a former synagogue, and it too is tiny, as museums go. But ironically, as the community has shrunk, the curators have sought to expand into adjoining properties, leading to a standoff with neighbours.

The plan involved demolition of the existing houses and three others, to allow a purpose-built exhibition space. And in another irony, the campaign against it is partly based on a desire by conservationists to preserve the old synagogue.

In any case, the impasse continues. As of 2015, visitors searching for the museum in the maze of Portobello's little streets are still being helped, inadvertently, by the banners on other houses campaigning against the expansion.

Address Walworth Road, Portobello, Dublin 8, Tel +353.(0)1.4531797, www.jewishmuseum.ie | **Getting there** Bus routes 16 or 122 to Harrington St; or Luas Green Line to Harcourt St, then a 7-minute walk | **Hours** May–Oct, Sun–Thu 11am–3.30pm; Nov–Apr, Sun 10.30am–2.30pm. Visits outside official opening hours can be made by appointment | **Tip** Note the plaque next door to the museum at the birthplace of Barry Fitzgerald, a Hollywood star who won an Oscar playing alongside Bing Crosby in the 1944 movie *Going My Way*.

49__The Irish Times Clock

Calling time on Brian O'Nolan's day job

The *Irish Times* clock is not just one of Dublin's best-known time-pieces, it's among the more mobile too. It has migrated from the newspaper's original site on Westmoreland Street, via a spell on D'Olier Street, to the current location. In the process, it has retained a reputation for punctuality, in contrast with another Dublin clock, which the paper once made infamous.

All traces of Andy Clarkin's coal merchants have long since disappeared from nearby Pearse Street. But back in the 1950s, the premises were known for their useless shopfront clock, which had been stopped for years. And when it remained stopped even after Clarkin became Dublin's Lord Mayor, it earned the wrath of the *Times* satirist, Myles na gCopaleen. Na gCopaleen was a pseudonym of Brian O'Nolan, a civil servant who also wrote novels as Flann O'Brien. His daily column, "Cruiskeen Lawn," excoriated official incompetence, of which Clarkin's clock became a favourite example.

Among other things, Myles encouraged readers to greet the mayor with a salute in the shape of its stopped hands. Over time he also reduced the campaign to a handy acronym, ACCISS – "Andy Clarkin's Clock is Still Stopped." Which, as well as being a deft summary, also served as an ingenious joke on the mayor's habit of mispronouncing the word *ask* and his undue deference in all things to his wife (named "Cis" for short).

In the end, however, the joke was on O'Nolan. Na gCopaleen's writings had often antagonised his political superiors. But he usually survived because of the pseudonym, and because the column was occasionally written by others. Unfortunately, his zeal in the Clarkin campaign led him to be photographed under the clock. The clipping was added to his civil service file. And soon afterwards, when his own government minister recognised himself as the butt of a Na gCopaleen joke, it was decreed that O'Nolan's time was up.

Address Junction of Tara Street and Townsend Street, Dublin 2 | Getting there All City Centre bus routes; DART rail to Tara St; or Luas Red Line to Abbey St, then a 5-minute walk | Tip For a good oral version of the Myles na gCopaleen stopped-clock campaign, hear actor Val O'Donnell's account on www.storymap.ie/flanns-final-fanfare.

50__ The Irish Whiskey Museum

Bottling history

You may notice a bit of a gold rush going on in Ireland these days, but unlike all past ones, it doesn't involve searching for metal. The gold in this case is liquid, and goes by the name of "whiskey." And although there are no large, hitherto-unknown deposits anywhere, the potential profits still make it an attractive prospect for those with money or patience.

The key to their optimism is Ireland's long and proven mastery of whiskey production. It probably invented the drink (the Scots might claim otherwise). Either way, until about a century ago it was the market leader, with Scotch the poor relation, until bad decisions and bad luck sent the local industry into a long decline and reversed the countries' positions. But now, with the global demand expanding as never before, Ireland is getting back into the game. New distilleries are opening everywhere, reclaiming historic know-how and provenance. In an area of Dublin once known as the "Golden Triangle" because it had three giant whiskey companies – all since closed or moved – a new distillery opened in 2015 and another is on the way.

The industry's story is the subject of the Irish Whiskey Museum, opened in 2015 and itself part of the revival. Among its exhibits is a sort of graph comprising old whiskey bottles, rising and falling and rising again along the walls. Guided tours lead, crucially, to a bar, where the modern-day brands can be tasted.

Judicious quotations are scattered along the way. They include Samuel Johnson's 1755 dictionary definition of *Usqueba'ugh* (an early Anglicisation of *uisce beatha*, or "water of life"): "It is a compounded distilled spirit … and the Irish sort is particularly distinguished for its pleasant and mild flavour. The Highland sort is somewhat hotter; and, by corruption, in Scottish they call it whisky."

Address 119 Grafton Street, Dublin 2, Tel +353.(0)1.5250970, www.irishwhiskeymuseum.ie | **Getting there** All City Centre bus routes | **Hours** Daily 10.30am–8pm. Admission: the "standard" tour costs €15 per adult (€13 for students and seniors) and includes three whiskey tastings; the "VIP" tour (€18 / €16) includes a tasting of aged whiskey and a souvenir | **Tip** After the whiskey museum, you might also like to visit the 125-year-old Fox's tobacconist shop next door.

51__The Irish Yeast Company

A shop that didn't rise

The Irish Yeast Company is one of the oldest shops in Dublin's city centre, and its unchanging presence on College Street, over many years, is a pleasant irony. While the rest of the city has been expanding, upwards and outwards, for the past century, the yeast shop has resolutely refused to grow, retaining its modest original proportions, like unleavened bread.

That said, its merchandise has changed with the times. In fact, despite the name, it doesn't sell all that much yeast anymore. The main line of business now is baking accessories: cake boards, moulds, trays, icing equipment, and decorative items. It boasts the widest range of bride and groom figurines anywhere. And as well as accessories for wedding cakes, it sells them for all the major anniversaries. But dating as it does from 1894, the Irish Yeast Company has lasted longer than any marriage ever will. In fact, its proprietor, John Moreland, who was born above the shop, has been working behind the counter for well over 70 years, having started in the family concern at age 16.

The surrounding area has been utterly transformed in the decades since, with hardly any other businesses remaining from that era. Moreland's wouldn't be around either, if he had accepted offers from developers in the 1990s. But as he told them, he didn't need the money, and he had no interest in moving anywhere else.

The Irish Yeast Company only opens for a few hours a day now. And it's not clear what will become of the place when Moreland is no longer here to operate it, although the old-fashioned shop frontage, with its ornate pilasters and landmark sign, will surely be preserved.

It's not the sort of shop you can easily browse in, unfortunately, unless you're a baker or you're planning a wedding. Even so, you should drop in if passing. The venerable proprietor is used to getting curious visitors.

CAKE DECORATIONS
CAKE PILLARS
CAKE BOARDS
CAKE CARDS

FINE SUGAR PASTE
For FLOWER MAKING

CAKE BOXES
10" — €3.00
12" — €3.50
14" — €4.00

EDIBLE
WAFER Ro

Address 6 College Street, Dublin 2, Tel +353.0(1).6778575 | Getting there All City
Centre bus routes; or DART rail to Tara St, then a 5-minute walk | Hours Mon,
Wed & Fri 2pm–5pm, Tue & Thu 10.30am–1.30pm | Tip While on College Street,
look for the nearby Long Stone sculpture: a replica of a Viking territorial marker that
stood at the same spot for almost a millennium, until it was stolen in the 1700s.

52_Isolde's Tower &
The Czech Inn

Where the new and old Dublin collide

Isolde's Tower and the Czech Inn make an odd couple at the western end of Temple Bar, but their juxtaposition is not without charm. The tower, or what little remains of it, is a leftover from the 13th-century city walls. The pub is a latter-day invader: its bad-pun name forgivable when you realise it specialises in Czech beer and is popular with eastern Europeans.

The tower was named after a 6th-century Irish princess: one of a pair of star-crossed lovers (the Cornish knight Tristan being the male half) whose story inspired Shakespeare and Wagner, among others. Her cult must have been strong in medieval Dublin, because the name is also preserved in the Liffey-side suburb of Chapelizod. The tower was located much further downriver. In fact, it was at the northeast corner of the city walls, making it especially important as the first line of defence against any hostile new arrivals who might sail into the Liffey from the seas beyond.

Its base was discovered during excavations in the 1990s, amid preparations for yet another new building in Temple Bar. Construction went ahead on condition that the ruins be incorporated into the development and made permanently accessible to public view. And so they were, after a fashion: left visible behind a metal grill that echoes the tower's design. Alas, the grill already looks rusted and shabby, and is often blocked by bins. But in truth, anyway, there's not that much to see through it. That's the problem with subterranean ruins: important as they are, they're usually not very exciting.

So, yes, the tower's base is worth a quick look. But after that, you'd be better off reading a history of the medieval city. And a good place to read it is the adjoining pub, which also used to be called Isolde's Tower, until it was renamed for some of the city's friendlier invaders.

Address Exchange Street Lower, Dublin 2 | **Getting there** Various bus routes, including 37, 39, 39 a, 70, and 83; or Luas Red Line to Jervis, then a 5-minute walk | **Tip** For an idea of what Isolde's Tower looked like when it was still intact, see the Record Tower (p. 172) in nearby Dublin Castle.

53_Iveagh Gardens

In the middle of Dublin, but a mystery to most

The world and its mother visit St Stephen's Green, the main public garden in central Dublin. But barely a three-minute walk away is another large park that sees nothing like that number of visitors. On some days, you could even have it to yourself.

The Iveagh Gardens are still a secret to many residents of the city, in part because they lack an obvious entrance. They lurk behind the stately buildings on the south side of Stephen's Green, but there's no way in from there. The main entry points are via the end of a cul-de-sac off Harcourt Street, on the west side, and from Hatch Street on the south; although there's also a small gateway hidden behind the National Concert Hall, a building with which the gardens were once intimately associated.

They owe their modern layout to the Great Exhibition of 1865, a sort of World's Fair, for which the concert hall was also constructed. Among their unusual features is a sunken grass rectangle, bigger than a football pitch but originally designed for the archery competitions that were part of the 1865 fair. This is said to be Ireland's only custom-built archery garden. But it's been a long time since arrows were fired there. The venue is now more likely to feature events like an annual mid-summer comedy festival, when pointed one-liners go zinging through the air instead.

Other features include a water cascade over a rock feature comprising pieces of each of Ireland's 32 counties. You can also lose yourself in a maze, although only if you're two feet tall. It's a miniature version of the one in Hampton Court, London.

There are a few interesting statues too, but just as the gardens are uncrowded by living people, they are also largely devoid of masonry. What they have, mainly, is green space and trees. This was in keeping with the wishes of their last private owner, Rupert Guinness, who gifted them to the State as an extra "lung" for Dublin.

Address Clonmel Street, Dublin 2, Tel +353.(0)1.4757816, www.iveaghgardens.ie | Getting there Various bus routes, including 14, 15, 15 a, 15 b, 44, 46 a, 61, and 140; or Luas Green Line to Harcourt St | Hours Dec & Jan, Mon–Sat 8am–3.30pm, Sun 10am–3.30pm; Feb & Nov, daily 8am–4pm; Mar–Oct, daily 8am–6pm | Tip Look for the sundial in the miniature maze, complete with brass plaques telling you how to convert sun time to clock time during the months when the sun is either "slow" or "fast."

54__ The James Joyce Tower
Built for war, borrowed by literature

The Martello Tower at Sandycove was one of about 50 built in Ireland during the Napoleonic Wars, 26 of them in a visually linked line along the coast of Dublin alone. Equipped with cannons, they were designed to repel an expected French invasion, and when the invasion didn't happen, they became historic curiosities. But thanks to one short-lived resident, the Martello at Sandycove is now one of the most famous addresses in world literature.

For six nights in September 1904, James Joyce lived in the tower, courtesy of his friend Oliver St John Gogarty, who was renting it from the State at £8 a year. Gogarty would later become a well-known surgeon, senator, writer, and wit. At the time, however, he was a medical student with a vague ambition to "Hellenise" Ireland (make it civilised, in the manner of ancient Greece).

Joyce was his uneasy ally in this crusade. But it was an incident involving another resident, Samuel Chevenix Trench, that brought the adventure to an abrupt end. Ironically, in a place where the original artillery had proved unnecessary, the story also involved gunfire.

Woken by a nightmare about a black panther, Trench started shooting at the pots and pans that hung over Joyce's bed, causing them to crash down on top of him. Joyce, who had not been getting on well with his housemates even before this, took this as a hint and left the next morning. The event propelled him into exile, although he was heading in that general direction anyway. He left Ireland shortly afterwards, for a life in Trieste, Paris, and finally Zurich, where he died.

His most famous work, *Ulysses*, is set on a single day in Dublin: 16 June 1904, when he first courted his future wife. But it begins in the Martello Tower, in the wake of the shooting incident, with Trench disguised as "Haines" and Gogarty as the man described in the book's opening words: "Stately, plump Buck Mulligan …"

Address James Joyce Tower and Museum, Sandycove Point, Sandycove, County Dublin, Tel +353.(0)1.2809265, www.jamesjoycetower.com | Getting there DART rail to Sandycove and Glasthule Station; or bus route 59 | Hours Daily 10am–6pm (10am–4pm in winter) | Tip The Joyce Tower is right beside the "Forty Foot" seaside bathing place, once reserved for "gentlemen" but now open to both sexes.

55_ The Jeanie Johnston

A famine memorial on water

Many of the people who left Ireland during the Great Famine did so in "coffin ships," so called because they were unhygienic, overcrowded, and lacking sufficient provisions, with passenger mortality rates as high as 30 percent. The original *Jeanie Johnston* wasn't one of those. In 16 voyages, starting in 1847, it brought 2500 Irish people to North America safely, without a single loss. Even when it sank in 1855, it went down so slowly that those on board were able to climb the rigging and stay there long enough to be rescued.

So when it was decided to build a floating monument to the Famine during the 1990s, the *Jeanie Johnston* was the model chosen. A traditional three-masted barque, its design details were compromised only by modern marine safety standards.

The reconstruction doubled as a peace project, involving young people from both Northern Ireland and the Republic, which was emerging from 30 years of the Troubles.

Unfortunately, the financial plan was not as well thought out as the ship. And in becoming a monument to a human catastrophe, the new *Jeanie Johnston* ironically also became a symbol of a lesser disaster: Ireland's property and banking crash of the early noughties.

By then the ship had massively overrun its budget, taking nine years to build, and eventually costing 14 million euros instead of the projected 4 million, most of it taxpayers' money. Worse still, after several successful voyages and then some years in dock, it was found insufficiently seaworthy for one possible use: as the new state sail-training vessel.

For now, the ship remains a floating, but not sailing, museum, and costs more to run than it can earn from visitors or corporate rentals. On the plus side, it's moored on the River Liffey next to the Irish Financial Services Centre, where it serves as a useful warning about the risks of insufficient oversight whenever large sums of money are involved.

Address Custom House Quay, Dublin 1, Tel +353.0(1).4730111, www.jeaniejohnston.ie | **Getting there** Bus routes 90 or 151; or Luas Red Line to George's Dock, then a 5-minute walk | **Hours** Daily, tours every half hour 10am–4.30pm | **Tip** On the quays near the ship is Rowan Gillespie's sculpture *Famine*, and the *World Poverty Stone*, by Stuart McGrath.

56___Kilmainham Gaol

A prison that became a shrine to Irish freedom

Traditionally, prisoners have been more likely to want to destroy their places of incarceration than preserve them. Kilmainham Gaol was different. When "Ireland's Bastille," by then closed and falling derelict, was threatened with demolition in the 1950s, it was the former inmates and other historically minded people who hatched a plot to save it.

They didn't need to dig any secret tunnels, except through bureaucracy. But once in, they restored the prison themselves, then handed it back to the State as a museum. Today it's a shrine to those who fought for Irish independence, especially the leaders of the 1916 Rising who were shot in its "Stone-breaker's Yard."

The long indecision about what to do with it was in part due to the fact that Ireland's independence struggle ended in civil war. The jail's last prisoners were Irishmen incarcerated by Irishmen, and in many cases executed by them. Much bitterness ensued. So when turning it into a museum, the restoration committee decided the only way forward was to ignore this period and present a united front in the story of Ireland's struggle for freedom. Half a century later, the ceasefire is still holding.

An indirect result of all the tourists now visiting the area is a Hilton Hotel located, with unintentionally witty juxtaposition, opposite the prison. Of course the gaol itself, built in 1796, is no longer in the accommodation business. And when it was, the rooms were rarely luxurious, although there were exceptions.

As an involuntary guest here from 1881–82, Irish nationalist leader Charles Stewart Parnell was kept in relative comfort, with an armchair and open fire, as he negotiated the terms of his release. But he was one of the luckier ones. As the museum explains, most of the prison's early inmates were in economy class, with up to five sharing a small cell, and only a candle for light or warmth.

Address Inchicore Road, Kilmainham, Dublin 8, Tel +353.(0)1.4535984, www.heritageireland.ie | Getting there Bus routes 13, 40, 69, or 79 | Tip Still off most tourists' radars, the Edwin Lutyens-designed War Memorial Gardens (see p. 220) at Islandbridge is but a 10-minute walk from Kilmainham Gaol.

57_Lady Lavery
A beauty who personified Ireland

It was long a tradition in Ireland that nationalist poets and playwrights depicted the country as a woman – a suffering woman, usually: sometimes young and beautiful, sometimes old and sad, and named variously as Dark Rosaleen, Róisín Dubh, or Cathleen ni Houlihan.

So when a newly independent Ireland finally got to print its own banknotes in the 1920s, it was decided that they too should feature this female personification of the nation's soul. Sure enough, for the next 50 years, Irish paper currency was adorned by the portrait of a frail beauty with red hair and big, soulful eyes, undimmed by centuries of poverty and oppression.

The irony is that the model for this ideal manifestation of Irishness was a Chicago-born socialite, Hazel Lavery (nee Martyn). Daughter of a wealthy industrialist, she had grown up as "the most beautiful girl in the Midwest." By the time she appeared on the banknotes, she was a Lady, living in a mansion in London.

The key to her role in Irish banking history was her second husband, Sir John Lavery, the Belfast artist commissioned for the job. His wife was his favourite subject. He painted her more often than Monet painted haystacks: most dramatically in *The Artist's Studio*, a large work on display in the National Gallery of Ireland.

It was only natural he should also make Hazel the model for a portrait that, in the joking words of then Irish leader W T Cosgrave, "every Irishman" would carry "next to his heart." In fact, speaking of hearts, she was linked romantically with two of Cosgrave's colleagues in the struggle for independence, although the rumours remain unsubstantiated.

Lady Lavery appeared on the banknotes until the late 1970s, when she was replaced by a series of historical and cultural figures. Even then, she continued to haunt the currency as a watermark, and only finally disappeared in 2002 with the introduction of the euro.

Address The National Gallery, Clare Street, Dublin 2, Tel +353.(0)1.6615133, www.nationalgallery.ie | **Getting there** Bus routes 4, 7, or 8; or DART rail to Pearse Station, then a 5-minute walk | **Hours** Mon–Thu & Sat 9.15am–5.30pm, Thu 9.15am–8.30pm, Sun 11am–5.30pm. Admission free | **Tip** Lavery's banknote portrait remains the property of the Central Bank but is on loan to the National Gallery. Another portrait can be seen at the Hugh Lane Gallery, on Parnell Square.

58__Leinster House

Where the Fighting Irish and the Talking Irish meet

Entering Leinster House, seat of Ireland's parliament, you pass two portraits facing each other across the lobby. One is of Michael Collins, guerrilla leader in the War of Independence and finance minister in the underground government of the period. The other is Cathal Brugha, also a revolutionary, and minister for defence in the same cabinet. Allies in the fight against British rule, they became enemies when republicans split over a peace treaty Collins helped negotiate. In the civil war that followed, the anti-treaty Brugha died in a hail of bullets from former comrades in July 1922. A month later, Collins was assassinated too, fulfilling his prediction that the treaty would be his "death warrant."

The portraits make a sombre entrance to the parliament that both men helped establish. So does the Latin inscription on the building's foundation stone, laid two centuries earlier in 1747, in which the architect imagined future visitors surveying the ruins of his work, and asked them to reflect on "how frail all things are, when such memorials of such men cannot outlive misfortune."

The mansion's modern role as home to Ireland's Houses of the Oireachtas has helped postpone that gloomy scenario. But ominously, for its current purpose, one of its former occupants described it as a "melancholy" place that did not "inspire the brightest ideas."

On the other hand, it is said to have inspired part of Washington's White House. And the late U.S. president John F Kennedy is among the more illustrious visitors who have addressed the Oireachtas over the years. On a 1963 visit, he left behind a memento that also highlights the dramatic contrast between the building's military past and its parliamentary present. It's a flag from the Union Army's famous Irish Brigade, the "Fighting 69th," who fought in the American Civil War – first presented in the 1860s to replace colours destroyed in battle, and still displayed proudly in Leinster House.

Address Kildare Street, Dublin 2, Tel +353.(0)1.16183271, www.oireachtas.ie | **Getting there** Various bus routes, including 7 b, 7 d, 11, 15 a, 15 b, 39 a, and 145; or Luas Green Line to St Stephen's Green, then a 10-minute walk | **Hours** There are only two ways to access Leinster House: at the invitation of your local TD or senator, or, more suitable for non-Irish visitors, by joining the "walk-up" tours held Mon & Fri 10.30am & 2.30pm. Book by email at event.desk@oireachtas.ie. Bring ID, arrive 15 minutes early, and avoid carrying bulky bags | **Tip** Note the traffic lights at the Dáil's Kildare-St entrance: a crossing much frequented by politicians returning to the house to vote and one of the few in Dublin where the pedestrian button works instantaneously every time.

59__ The Liberties
The beating heart of Dublin

The part of Dublin known as the "Liberties" contains several of the city's most visited places, including Christchurch, St Patrick's Cathedral, and that mother of all tourist attractions, the Guinness Storehouse. But crammed as it is with colour and character, the area is worth touring in its own right, preferably on foot.

One problem is how to define it, exactly. Historically, the Liberties were a number of self-governing locales allied to but outside the walled city. Today, the term is loosely applied to the narrow streets east of St Patrick's and south of the Guinness Brewery, with a fuzzy boundary somewhere north of the South Circular Road.

The area was for centuries dominated by weavers: originally Huguenot refugees from France, who prospered for a time, building the "Dutch Billy" houses that once typified Dublin before Georgian architecture took over. But the trade was gradually reduced by protectionist English laws and other setbacks and is today preserved only in place names, including Weavers Square.

By the 19th century, the Liberties had levels of overcrowding and poverty that horrified foreign travel writers. The area was also a centre of revolution, most famously in 1803, when a young lawyer named Robert Emmet led a doomed uprising on Thomas Street. He was hanged and beheaded at the scene of his crime, outside St Catherine's Church, where a plaque now marks the spot.

The Liberties include Meath Street, bustling with pavement traders and market arcades, and Francis Street, where the city's antique dealers congregate. Another, increasingly important, place is Newmarket Square, long run down but now the scene of a major revival, with a new distillery and several markets.

The Liberties are also one of the last remaining parts of Dublin where working horses are still stabled, although these days they're more likely to be hauling tourists than cartloads of coal.

Address A map of the area is available at www.libertiesdublin.ie, Tel +353.(0)1.2225180 | **Getting there** Various bus routes including 13, 49, 123, 150, and 151 | **Hours** The Dublin Food Co-op (www.dublinfood.coop) in Newmarket Square: Thu–Sun. The Green Door Market (thegreendoor.ie): Thu–Sat. The Dublin Flea Market in Newmarket Square: last Sun of each month | **Tip** In late 2015, the city council announced plans for a new park in the Liberties, the city's first in 100 years, with work beginning in 2016.

60__The Liffey Boardwalk

A (mostly) pleasant refuge from the traffic-crazed quays

In contrast with the more gently sloped city riverbanks of the Seine or the Danube, the steep-walled sides of Dublin's Liffey are not well suited to strolling. The city quays that run alongside are for the most part choked with cars and buses, and the footpaths, especially near the city centre's O'Connell Bridge, are intimidatingly narrow and close to the traffic.

A partial solution, built to mark the millennium year 2000, is the Liffey Boardwalk, which now stretches for about a third of a mile beside the busiest quays, on the river side of the walls.

The development was notable, among other things, for being on the Northside. The Liffey is Dublin's most famous social divider, separating the supposedly impoverished Northsiders from their well-heeled neighbours to the south (a gross simplification, with a grain of truth, in which both communities manage to take equal pride).

But the Northside did have one big thing to recommend it as the location for the boardwalk: exposure to whatever sunshine comes the city's way. So on balmier days, the walkway can be a very pleasant place to stroll, or to sit and drink a coffee from one of its vending stalls.

Unfortunately, another kind of shadow has encroached in the years since it opened. Some of Dublin's many drug users have taken to frequenting it – particular the section east of O'Connell Bridge. It's popular with winos too, and the benches are often a temporary resting place for the homeless.

Even so, the boardwalk is as safe as most parts of the city, especially during the day. If you don't like the look of a section, you can always revert to the footpaths on the other side of the wall. Like a typical Dublin conversation, the boardwalk is frequently interrupted: there are no fewer than five bridges along its short length, with the walkway forced to make exits and entrances on either side.

Address The Liffey Boardwalk runs between Grattan Bridge and Butt Bridge, Dublin 1 | Getting there Various bus routes; or Luas Red Line to Abbey St or Jervis, then a 3-minute walk | Tip The boardwalk is among the best viewing points for the Liffey Swim, held annually – usually in September – since 1920.

61__The Little Museum of Dublin

Holding up a small mirror to the city

Among the more obscure exhibits in the Little Museum of Dublin is the first issue of a forgotten Irish magazine from 1999 that now serves as a cautionary tale for future generations. It was called *Nouveau*, and was aimed shamelessly at the nouveau riche, of which Dublin had unprecedented numbers at the time, thanks to the Celtic Tiger economy. The magazine was full of advice for people who had more money than they knew what to do with, including articles on art investment, offshore gambling, Harley Davidson motorbikes, and "skiing with the rich."

Not surprisingly, the editor was confident of success. In a breezy introduction, he declared the risks of publishing to be "minimal." He was wrong. There was no second issue, suggesting that, as rampantly consumerist as Ireland may have been then, it had not completely – in the local phrase – lost the run of itself.

The crash that followed was one of the worst in European history. But there was a silver lining to the collapse in property prices, of which the Little Museum (established 2011) is proof. Small though it may be, it occupies three storeys of a fine house on St Stephen's Green, within a stone's throw of the sky-high rents of Grafton Street. In the boom economy, such a location would not have been affordable.

The museum collection concentrates on the life of the city since 1900, a time of huge political and economic change, but does so in a charmingly random way, with a clutter of colourful details rather than big pictures.

Less miniature exhibits include "the editor's office," built around the desk of a famously eccentric *Irish Times* editor, Bertie Smyllie; and the Alfie Byrne room, dedicated to an extraordinarily popular politician who was elected Lord Mayor of Dublin 10 times.

Address 15 St Stephen's Green, Dublin 2, Tel +353.(0)1.6611000, www.littlemuseum.ie | Getting there Various bus routes, including 7 b, 7 d, 11, 25 a, 25 b, 38 a, 38 b, and 39; or Luas Green Line to St Stephen's Green | Hours Daily 9.30am–5pm, Thu open till 8pm. Admission: €4.50–€7; Thu 6pm–8pm free | Tip You can make your own way around the museum, but to get a sense of the exhibits, especially if you're not a Dubliner, a guided tour is highly recommended. The basement houses the cafe Hatch & Sons Irish Kitchen.

62___ The Magazine Fort
A 300-year-old ruin that nearly went out with a bang

When the rulers of an impoverished Ireland decided to build a magazine fort for storing weapons and gunpowder in 1734, Dublin's famous satirist Jonathan Swift was unimpressed. He wrote, in verse: "Now here's a proof of Irish sense / Here Irish wit is seen / When nothing's left that's worth defence / We build a magazine."

The project went ahead anyway, on St Thomas' Hill in Phoenix Park, until then the seat of English rule in Ireland as the home of the Viceroys, who now decamped to a new site further north. In fact, this had also been the location of an even older house, Phoenix Lodge, which gave what is now the largest city park in Europe its name: from a corruption of the Irish *fionn uisce* ("clear water").

The Magazine Fort survived for more than two centuries, although it nearly came to a spectacular end during the 1916 Rising, when insurgents attempted to blow up the explosives, only for the fuse to sputter out.

Two decades later, just before Christmas 1939, the paramilitary Irish Republican Army took advantage of seasonal relaxation in security to raid the fort, making off with 13 truckloads of ammunition. They were victims of their own success. The logistics of hiding the material so overwhelmed the small, illegal organisation that most of it was quickly recovered. But the fort had outlived its usefulness and was closed soon afterwards.

Today the huge, star-shaped structure is an abandoned, crumbling ruin. The hillsides sloping down from it are now used mainly as an assault course for cross-country runners and boot-campers, as is the nearby Khyber Road.

Other than that, the old fort no longer serves a function. But you can still walk around its defensive moat on a well-worn path, and it offers a pleasant vantage point from which to view both this corner of the park and the nearby Liffey Valley.

Address Military Road, Phoenix Park, Dublin 8, Tel +353.(0)1.8205800, www.phoenixpark.ie | **Getting there** Bus routes 25 and 26 to Islandbridge Gate | **Hours** Always open. Admission free | **Tip** Compare the panorama of the city now with William Ashford's *A View of Dublin from Chapelizod*, painted near here in 1797 and on display in the National Gallery of Ireland (Merrion Square W, Dublin 2).

63 Margaret Naylor's Grave

The war tragedy of a star-crossed couple

Among the British soldiers and their relatives buried in Grangegorman Military Cemetery, there is one grave, dated 1916, that marks a tragic coincidence. It contains the remains of Margaret Naylor, a Dublin housewife and mother of three, who, on the morning of April 29 of that year, left her home in search of bread.

This was a dangerous mission, because four days earlier, Irish nationalists had seized key buildings in the city and declared a republic. Dublin was now at war, with soldiers and rebels firing at each other from rooftops and many civilians caught in the crossfire. Margaret Naylor was among the unlucky. Walking across Ringsend Drawbridge, she was shot in the head, and died two days later.

Unaware of this, meanwhile, her husband, John, was in the trenches of Northern France. A grocery-shop porter, he had joined the Royal Dublin Fusiliers after the outbreak of the First World War. And on the day his wife was fatally wounded back home, he had the misfortune to be in a place called Hulluch, near Loos, when the Germans launched a cloud-gas attack on Allied lines.

Naylor was one of several hundred soldiers to die from the effects of chlorine and phosgene, said to have been like "drowning on dry land." He is presumed buried near the battlefield, but the location is now unknown. His name is commemorated on a memorial wall at Loos.

His wife, by contrast, was buried in the regimental cemetery in Dublin. But as the British military service became an inconvenient memory in post-war Ireland, by then struggling towards independence, her grave too was soon forgotten.

By the end of the 20th century, descendants of the Naylors didn't know where Margaret was buried either. Then a grandson tracked down the location. Now a new headstone marks both the grave and the poignant coincidence of her husband's almost-simultaneous death, several hundred miles away in France.

Address Grangegorman Military Cemetery, Blackhorse Avenue, Dublin 7, Tel +353.(0)1.8213021 (Heritage Ireland), www.opwdublincommemorative.ie | Getting there Bus route 37 | Hours Daily 10am–4pm | Tip The military cemetery is a short distance from Ireland's "longest pub," the Hole in the Wall (Blackhorse Ave, Dublin 7).

64 The Marino Casino

An architectural masterpiece in miniature

Contrary to what its name might suggest, the Marino Casino is a not a place for gambling. The confusion has a certain aptness however. The building is, in one sense, a monument to a man who had more money than he knew what to do with. And he sank so much into it – up to £40,000 in the 1750s – that it became a great burden on the family estate.

Even so, the Casino (Italian for "little house") is considered a masterpiece of its genre: architecture for architecture's sake. And unlike most follies of the era, its beauty wasn't entirely useless.

Although it appears from the outside to contain only one room, it actually has no fewer than 16, on three floors. The huge entrance door and the large windows are carefully constructed shams, disguising servants' quarters, a state bedroom, and spaces wherein an aristocrat could host parties, albeit small ones.

From ornate ceiling plasterwork to parquet floors featuring some of the world's most rare types of wood, the Casino is crammed with exquisite detail. Sometimes form and function are combined ingeniously, as in the hollowed-out columns that double as downpipes.

The man who commissioned it, James Caulfield, aka the Earl of Charlemont, conceived the idea during a nine-year "grand tour" of Italy and Greece. In love with all things Italian on his return, he renamed his sea-facing estate "Marino," which now describes the surrounding suburb.

Alas, he lived to see a spiteful rival build a tall terrace, Marino Crescent (birthplace of Bram Stoker), across his view. And after all the money he lavished on it, the house was underappreciated by his descendants. It had fallen into neglect by the time a cardinal bought the estate for a school in 1878. But it wasn't until the government took over the Casino 40 years later, and eventually began refurbishing it, that the future of this extraordinary miniature was secured.

Address Cherrymount Crescent, off Malahide Road, Marino, Dublin 3, Tel +353.(0)1.8331618 | **Getting there** Various bus routes, including 14, 27, 27 a, 27 b, 42, 43, and 128 | **Hours** June–Sep, daily 10am–6pm, May & Oct, daily 10am–5pm. Last entry 45 minutes before closing. Admission: €2–€4 | **Tip** A private residence, unmarked by any plaque, Bram Stoker's birthplace is at No 15, Marino Crescent, a 10-minute walk from the Casino.

65 Marsh's Library

Three centuries of scholarship, occasionally interrupted

Founded in 1701, Marsh's is the oldest library in Ireland and one of the country's few 18th-century buildings still serving its original purpose. Scholars are no longer locked in its cages to prevent them stealing books. But the cages are still there, as are the original oak cases, and the library has hardly changed in 300 years.

For most of that time it has been a safe haven for scholarship, hidden away in St Patrick's Close. Not so, however, for one brief period in April 1916. During the Easter Rising by Irish republicans, the building found itself in the front line between the nearby rebel garrison at Jacob's Biscuit Factory and British soldiers firing machine guns from St Patrick's Park.

One fusillade of bullets strafed a window, "injuring," as the library's management put it, "five books." The small holes can still be seen in the spines. More chillingly, the progress of the bullets can be traced through the dense pagination towards their larger "exit wounds."

There are very old books among Marsh's 25,000-strong collection, including a volume of Cicero's letters published in 1472. And some very famous students have studied them throughout the centuries: Jonathan Swift (who was Dean of the cathedral next door), Bram Stoker, and James Joyce, to name a few.

Like the bullets of 1916, if not quite so violently, Swift too left his mark on the collection, albeit via books he himself owned. On a history of the 1715 Scots rebellion, for example, he ranted in the margins: "Cursed abominable, hellish Scottish villains, everlasting traitors."

But then, the great satirist was a man of strong opinions. Not even Archbishop Narcissus Marsh, the library's founder, was immune from them. Writing when Marsh was near retirement, Swift suggested he had done little with his great advantages in life. He added: "No man will be either glad or sorry at his death, except his successor."

Address St Patrick's Close, Dublin 8, www.marshlibrary.ie, Tel +353.(0)1.4543511 | Getting there Various bus routes, including 27, 56 a, 151, and 77 a | Hours Mon & Wed–Fri 9.30am–5pm, Sat 10am–5pm; closed Tue, Sun, and bank holidays | Tip Jacob's Factory, for which the bullets that hit Marsh's were meant, is now the Irish National Archives, with an entrance on nearby Bishop Street.

66__McNeill's Pub

A musical twist on the Charge of the Light Brigade

The Charge of the Light Brigade (1854) has gone down in history as an outstanding example both of soldiers' courage and officers' incompetence. Tennyson's famous poem concentrated on the courage. The case for incompetence was summed up by a watching French marshal, who said: *C'est magnifique, mais ce n'est pas la guerre* ("It's magnificent, but it is not war").

Historians still dispute who was to blame for the confused orders that sent 673 British cavalrymen into a frontal assault against Russian artillery in what became the most notorious single incident of the Crimean War.

But in any case, between the orders and the charge, there had to be a bugle call. And it's a little-remembered fact, even in Ireland, that both the bugle and bugler were from Dublin. There is some debate too, in fact, as to whether William Brittain ever did sound the charge, or whether the cavalry jumped the gun after his signals to "walk," "trot," and "gallop." Unfortunately, he wasn't around long to clarify the matter, being one of the 118 British troops to die during the assault, or soon afterwards.

The bugle, which he clung to even as he fell, also suffered damage when a Russian on horseback tried to pick it up with his lance and punched a hole in it. It survived to go home with the other war-wounded and is now in a museum in England.

The instrument was made by John McNeill, a Dublin master craftsman, whose name is on the bugle and whose family business was based for many years at 140 Capel Street. The shop closed eventually, and then was revived for a time above a pub of the same name (but different ownership). Now there's just the pub. The good news is that this maintains the link with its heritage by hosting regular music sessions, although it tends to be Irish traditional music, which is strings-led. You're unlikely ever to hear a bugle there, which may be no bad thing.

Address 140 Capel Street, Dublin 1, Tel +353.(0)1.8747679, Facebook: McNeills Pub Sessions, Capel St | Getting there Luas Red Line to Jervis, then a 2-minute walk | Hours Mon–Thu 10am–11.30pm, Fri & Sat 10am–12.30am, Sun noon–11pm | Tip The Irish experience of the Crimean War is part of a permanent exhibition, "Soldiers and Chiefs," at the National Museum, Collins Barracks.

67 __ Meath Street

Dear old Dublin at its cheapest

There's nothing remotely touristy about Meath Street, the commercial heart of Dublin's old Liberties district. In fact, vast numbers of tourists descend on the area every day, but they're invariably heading to Guinness' Brewery, just a block away. Not many stop en route. And yet, partly for this reason, Meath Street provides the quintessential Dublin marketplace experience: busy, brash, and colourful, but unselfconsciously so, and with too much grittiness ever to lend itself to picture postcards.

The mix of shops is eclectic, to put it mildly. All the food you need is here, thanks to greengrocers, bakers, fishmongers, and butchers selling parts of animals you won't get in posher neighbourhoods: beef hearts, chicken gizzards, pigs' feet, pigs' tails, pigs' tongues. There's also a plethora of hair salons and beauty parlours. And catering (mainly) to the other gender, in an impoverished area, there is at least one betting shop too many, a casino, and several pubs.

But there are charities, too, a community centre, and a strong religious presence. Thus, close by a market called the New Dandelion is the Guild of the Little Flower: a drop-in named after St Therese, supplying meals and other services to the poor. Several businesses bear the historic prefix "Liberty." But this doesn't imply that anything is free here, only cheap. Even the Little Flower centre has traditionally charged diners a nominal amount ("penny dinners"), if they can afford it, to remove the stigma of handouts.

And it's because the bottom line matters so much there that, having been untouched by the Celtic Tiger boom, Meath Street has nevertheless suffered from the subsequent crash. The giant German discount stores, especially Lidl, now drain its customer base. Many shops have closed. But the area has suffered worse things, including a drug epidemic, and is famously resilient. It will survive a mere downturn.

Address Meath Street, Dublin 8 | Getting there Bus routes 13, 40, 51, 77, 121, or 123; Luas Green Line to St Stephen's Green, then a 10-minute walk; or Red Line to Four Courts, then a 10-minute walk | Tip For cut-price fabric and fashions, the Liberty Market (Thu–Sat only, from 10am) is hard to beat. And if you have a knitter in your life, check out Larry Mooney's wool stall in particular.

68_Monkstown Church

A building ahead of its time

Monkstown Anglican Church was much loved by Sir John Betjemen, the English poet and diplomat, who spent the Second World War in neutral Dublin, as a British press attaché-*cum*-spy. By some accounts, it may even have been his favourite church anywhere. But if it was, his affection for it put him in a small minority.

Built in 1830, Monkstown Church was the work of architect John Semple, better known in Dublin for the "Black Church," which achieved an unwanted notoriety among those with overactive imaginations. His work in Monkstown was notorious too, but only for its design, which was both ahead of its time and – in the view of some critics – in the wrong country.

Certainly the "Portuguese Gothic" architecture, set off these days by a tall palm tree on the approach road, would not look out of place in Goa or Mozambique. The design must have seemed even more radical when it first appeared. And sure enough, according to the church's website, there were savage early reviews.

One sensitive critic, from the *Dublin Penny Journal*, implied that it hurt him to look at it. Never had he seen "a greater perversion of judgment and taste," he wrote, adding that there was "not a spot in the church where the eye [could] rest without pain." That was in 1834. But in 1857, another commentator suggested that to anyone acquainted with the principles of religious architecture, the church "cannot but appear simply hideous." And another generation later, in 1880, it was still being damned (in the *Ecclesiastical Gazette*) as not "suitable for a Christian place of worship."

It wasn't until 80 years later, and Betjemen, that the tide of criticism began to turn. "Bold, modern, vast, and original," the poet called it. He added: "Only today is the … genius of Semple beginning to be appreciated." That was in 1958. More than half a century later, appreciation is not yet universal.

Address Monkstown Road, Monkstown Village, County Dublin, Tel +353.(0)1.2147714, www.monkstownparishchurch.ie | **Getting there** Bus routes 7, 8, or 75; or DART rail to Monkstown Station | **Hours** See website for church services | **Tip** A 300-metre walk from the church, on Carrickbrennan Road, are the picturesque ruins of the 15th-century Monkstown Castle.

69__Monto

Where Dublin switched off the red light

The author of *Ulysses* and *Finnegans Wake* lived at an estimated 20 different addresses during his years in Dublin, but the one now known as James Joyce Street wasn't one of them. The name is instead an indirect reference to the surrounding area's former notoriety, of which its modern offices and apartment blocks now give no other hint.

Between about 1850 and 1920, this part of the north inner city was Europe's biggest red-light district, nicknamed "Monto" after its main drag, Montgomery Street. By one count, in 1868, it had 132 brothels employing 1600 prostitutes. Their clientele ranged widely. The future King Edward VII, then Prince of Wales, is said to have lost his virginity there. Joyce was a customer too.

Monto is the setting of *Ulysses'* longest chapter: a mixture of reality and fantasy that ends with Stephen Dedalus (the character based on the author) getting into a drunken fight with a British soldier. Like many parts of the book, this was inspired by a real event. And indeed, the large military presence in Dublin – then the second city of the empire – was a mainstay of Monto's existence.

So when the Irish won their independence in 1921 and the British army left, Monto was one of the first targets for Catholic religious reformers. Backed by police raids, they effectively closed the area down between 1923 and 1925. Slum clearances finished the job. You have to look very hard now to find any traces of the neighbourhood's former life.

Ireland's post-independence moral crusade wasn't confined to brothels. There was strict censorship of books, magazines, and films, too. And when first published in 1922, in fact, *Ulysses* was too risqué even for the UK, where it was initially banned, and the US, where it was prosecuted for indecency. Ironically it was never censored in Ireland. It simply wasn't sold there for many years.

Address The area formerly known as Monto is bounded by Talbot Street, Amiens Street, Gardiner Street, and Seán MacDermott Street | Getting there Various bus routes; or Luas Red Line to Connolly Station | Tip The popular Dublin ballad "Monto" is a witty summary of the area's former notoriety, with language and references suggesting that the lyrics were composed circa 1900, during the area's heyday. In fact, the song was written in the 1960s by musician George "Hoddy" Hodnett, jazz critic for the *Irish Times*.

70 Mulligans Pub

Where Joyce meets journalism (and journalism wins)

Mulligans Pub has a long association with journalism, and with one newspaper firm in particular. For many years it was almost next door to the Irish Press group, which published daily, evening, and Sunday titles, all well lubricated by the Poolbeg Street bar.

Alas, the company went out of business in the 1990s. So among the relics on Mulligans' walls is a framed final edition of the *Evening Press*, signed by Con Houlihan, a gentle giant who had migrated from Kerry many years before to become one of Dublin's best-loved columnists. Now dead, he is himself the subject of a virtual shrine in the pub, including a framed photograph of him drinking his trademark concoction: a glass of brandy and milk.

But Houlihan is by no means the most famous journalist ever to drink in Mulligans. That title belongs, probably, to a young American reporter who turned up one day in 1947. His name was John F Kennedy. And it's said he was researching the pub's connections with James Joyce. Those connections are real enough, although not as auspicious as Mulligans might like. In fact, the pub's website implies that Joyce may have written some of *Ulysses* while sitting in the bar.

But not only does this seem unlikely – he left Ireland in 1912, never to return, and wrote his masterpiece in exile between 1914 and 1921 – it also draws attention to an embarrassing fact. In a book renowned for name-checking Dublin businesses of its era, *Ulysses* does not mention Mulligans.

Where the pub does feature is in Joyce's short story "Counterparts." And that's a dubious compliment. "Counterparts" is a bleak tale about a man who has a row with his boss, then pawns his watch for a night of drinking he can't afford, before going home and beating his son.

All told, Mulligans might be on safer ground with the journalists. But where it also excels, by common consent, is in serving some of Dublin's best Guinness.

Address 8 Poolbeg Street, Dublin 2, Tel +353.0(1).6775582, www.mulligans.ie |
Getting there DART rail to Tara St; or bus routes 68, 68a, or 69 to Burgh Quay | Hours
Mon–Thu 10am–11.30pm, Fri–Sat 10am–12.30am, Sun 12.30pm–11pm | Tip
Mulligans apart, Poolbeg Street's other main distinction is being in the shadow of Hawkins
House, headquarters of the Department of Health, but considered by many Dubliners to be
the city's ugliest building.

71 Napoleon's Toothbrush

A brush with greatness

When Napoleon departed for his final exile on St Helena, he brought with him an Irish surgeon, Barry O'Meara. And it is to Dr O'Meara that Dublin owes one of its more eccentric attractions: a small collection of Napoleonic relics, including a toothbrush, two snuff boxes, and a lancet used to bleed the by then ailing emperor.

The hoard is complemented by what may or may not be a tiny piece of Napoleon's coffin, mounted weirdly between the antlers of a miniature deer head. The provenance of that artefact is more uncertain, however: the Royal College of Physicians, home to these treasures, doesn't quite vouch for it.

O'Meara was a surgeon in the British naval service when he met his celebrity patient on board the HMS *Bellerophon*, where Napoleon surrendered after Waterloo. For the next three years on St Helena, he provided the Frenchman not just with medical supervision, but also with urbane company, a scarce commodity on the South Atlantic island. In return, the emperor suggested he keep a diary, for publication after his (Napoleon's) death. It would make a fortune, the emperor predicted. And he was right, eventually, although in the meantime, O'Meara did everything he could to keep his patient alive as long as possible.

In fact, his insistence that Bonaparte was being ill treated on St Helena earned him the enmity of the island's British governor, an early return home, and eventual dismissal from the navy, with the loss of his pension. But back in London, he reinvented himself as a private dentist, again with Napoleon's help. A letter of recommendation from the emperor was displayed in his window. So, even more impressively, was an imperial wisdom tooth he had extracted (alas, the tooth is not part of the Dublin collection).

When Napoleon died, in 1821, the doctor was finally able to publish his diaries. As predicted, they won him both wealth and fame.

Address Royal College of Physicians (RCPI), 6 Kildare Street, Dublin 2, www.rcpi.ie | **Getting there** Various bus routes to Kildare St and Nassau St; or Luas Green Line to St Stephen's Green, then a 10-minute walk | **Hours** Mon – Fri 9am – 5pm | **Tip** Just down the street from the RCPI, look out for the unusual animal carvings on the façade of Nos 2 and 3 – including a group of monkeys playing billiards.

72___The National Print Museum

Where they mind their p's and q's

With impeccable aptness, Ireland's National Print Museum is housed in a chapel: the deconsecrated garrison chapel of the former Beggars Bush army barracks. This echoes a centuries-old practice whereby trade unions in printing and journalism were organised in units called "chapels," which in turn reflected the fact that the first publishing houses in Britain and Ireland, in the 15th century, were attached to abbeys.

And there must have been something monklike about printers up to modern times, judging by one of the museum's smaller exhibits: a contract for an apprentice dated 1935. It committed the young man to seven years complete obedience to his employer, during which time he would neither "commit fornication, nor contract matrimony." He would also avoid "cards, dice-tables, or any unlawful games." Furthermore, he would not "haunt or use taverns, ale-houses, or play-houses." In return for all that restraint, he would be compensated to the tune of "10 shillings a week."

The trade was still at its height in 1935, and for another 50 years afterwards. Then the rise of computers made printers' skills obsolete within a generation.

So the museum is a re-creation of past glories. But oddly, for a profession that prided itself on accuracy, giving us the phrase "to mind your p's and q's," its star exhibit (on loan) is a botched job. It's a rare survivor of 1000 original copies of the 1916 Proclamation, printed in constrained circumstances by Irish republican rebels, who ran short of letters and had to improvise. But p's and q's were not the problem. Lowercase e's an o's were. The rebels had to run the posters off in two halves and use several fonts, while also turning a capital F into an E with sealing wax, among other idiosyncrasies. The imperfections didn't matter. Surviving copies now sell for six-figure sums.

Address Beggars Bush Barracks, Haddington Road, Dublin 4, Tel +353.(0)1.6603770, www.nationalprintmuseum.ie | **Getting there** Bus routes 4 or 7; or DART rail to Lansdowne Rd or Grand Canal Dock, then a 5-minute walk | **Hours** Mon–Fri 9am–5pm, Sat & Sun 2pm–5pm | **Tip** Guided tours are normally €3.50 for adults and €7 for families, but there's a free tour every Sunday at 3pm.

73__Newman House

A clash of cultures on St Stephen's Green

The second most notorious former resident of 86 St Stephen's Green was Richard Chapell Whaley, who died in 1769. A member of parliament, he was known for his dislike of religion, and in particular for a tendency to set fire to Catholic places of worship, which in time saw his name popularly amended to Richard "Burn-Chapel" Whaley. So it was richly ironic when, a century after his death, No 86 was acquired by Cardinal John Henry Newman to become the first Catholic University of Ireland, with a church next door for good measure.

In the meantime, however, Whaley had been exceeded in infamy by his son, Thomas "Buck" Whaley, who also became a member of parliament, but whose main professions, insofar as he had any, were gambling and debauchery. He once famously travelled to Jerusalem to win a wager. And it was a story widely circulated in Dublin at the time that, to win another bet, he had charged out of an upstairs window of No 86 on horseback and leapt over a carriage parked below onto mattresses he had placed on the street to break his fall.

In fact, according to his own memoirs, he performed that stunt in the English city of York. But in general, as one commentator put it, he "plunged with a natural relish into the vortex of bravado which distinguished the world of high life in the Irish capital at the time."

This is in stark contrast with another, later resident of No 86, the English poet and priest Gerard Manley Hopkins. Sent to Dublin to teach classical studies in 1884, he was a gentle sort who would not have enjoyed the city of Buck Whaley and his kind. Unfortunately, he didn't like the 1880s version either. "I have been warmly welcomed and most kindly treated," he wrote home. "But Dublin itself is a joyless place … I had fancied it quite different. The Phoenix Park is fine, but inconveniently far off. There are a few fine buildings …"

Address 85–86 St Stephen's Green South, Dublin 2, Tel +353.(0)1.7167422, www.ucd.ie | **Getting there** All cross-city bus routes; or Luas Green Line to St Stephen's Green or Harcourt St, then a 3-minute walk | **Hours** Guided tours of Newman House are held June, July, & August, Tue–Fri, at 2pm, 3pm, & 4pm | **Tip** If you can't get into No 86, or even if you can, you should visit the University Church next door, unique in Dublin for its Byzantine-style interior.

74_ The Old Airport Terminal
A modernist masterpiece and a relic of air travel past

If you're one of the millions of people who fly into Dublin with no-frills Ryanair, ironically, among the first things you see may be the relic of an era when air travel was much more glamorous (and expensive) than it is now.

The "Skybridge" that leads from Pier D, where many Ryanair planes arrive, curves around the original airport terminal, which was completed in 1941 and considered Ireland's first modernist building.

Influenced by Le Corbusier, the four-storey structure is itself curved, cleverly, with the short side gathering in intending passengers and the long side opening onto the runways, and the world.

Confusingly, according to the airport website, its curves and tiered floors were supposed to "echo the lines of a great ocean liner." But seen from above, in combination with the landscaping, it was also designed to look like a plane.

In what was still a poor country then, the terminal's construction was a gesture of confidence about its role in the expanding world of air travel. Ireland had already featured, albeit by accident, in several aviation milestones, including Alcock and Brown's first transatlantic flight and the more infamous one by Douglas "Wrong Way" Corrigan.

But opening at an inauspicious time, the airport experienced very quiet years in the early 1940s, with only a biweekly service to Liverpool. An expanded terminal soon followed, however. And by 2010, the gleaming Terminal 2 had been added, increasing capacity to 30 million passengers a year.

The good news is that the old building, redolent of an era when stewardesses dispensed unlimited in-flight hospitality in return for sky-high fares, is still in use. The bad news is that you can't visit it, except during "Open House" weekends. Happily, however, you may at least stop and admire it while using one of Ireland's latest gifts to European aviation: the low-cost, glamour-free flight.

Address Collinstown, County Dublin, Tel +353.(0)1.8141111, www.dublinairport.com | Getting there Bus routes 16, 41, 102, or Airlink 747 | Tip Tours of the old terminal are usually available during the annual Open House Dublin event, held in October. Visit www.openhousedublin.ie.

75__ The Old Dublin Lion House

A roaring success story

The "Celtic Tiger" was only a metaphor: a description of the economic boom Ireland experienced in the early years of the 21st century. But long before the country had a Tiger economy, it also had a lion one, and that was no mere figure of speech.

Between 1857 and the 1960s, the so-called "Irish lion industry" was a world leader in the breeding of these animals: famous not just for the prolific numbers produced – 600 in a century – but also for their size and strength. The operation was based in Dublin Zoo, where a sign on the former Lion House (now an aviary) hints at one of the secrets of the breeding project: the animals' "occasional diet of boiled potatoes and medicinal doses of whiskey punch." There may have been other distinctively local touches too, like the time – circa 1900 – when a litter of abandoned cubs had to be foster-mothered by what a visiting journalist called "a very beautiful Irish Red Setter."

In any case, the industry became a roaring success, in every sense. Dublin lions were much in demand from other zoos and were traded like modern football players. One recorded transaction involved the sale of two cubs for £200 "in part consideration of a pair of elephants."

The lion was of course a symbol of the British Empire, then at its height. But the Dublin breeding industry survived the transition to independence in 1921. It may even have had its crowning glory in the years afterwards, thanks to another then booming industry. According to a plausible if now unverifiable story, the first Metro-Goldwyn-Mayer lion was from Dublin. Originally named Cairbre, after a mythical Irish hero, he was exported to the States, where he became the less poetic "Slats." It's said he was hired to play Leo, the first MGM lion, from 1924 to 1928. If so, he was also unique in being the only one that didn't roar. His part, like the films then, was silent.

Dublin Zoo Heritage Trail

The Roberts House
Teach Roberts

The Roberts House is the oldest animal house in Dublin Zoo and was built for the lions when they were regarded as the most important species in the Zoo. Dublin's lions were sought after by zoos and dealers around the world. They generated much needed income and contributed positively to Dublin Zoo's international reputation.

The Roberts House was opened in 1902 and was named in honour of Field Marshal Lord Frederick Roberts, president of the Royal Zoological Society of Ireland from 1898 to 1902.

In 1947, Stephen the lion did a screen test for the MGM logo but the footage was never used. It is possible, however, that a Dublin Zoo lion was used in the MGM logo during the 1920s.

Left: Zoo council members inspecting the new lion house with Christopher Flood, lion keeper, 1902

Right: Field Marshal Lord Frederick Roberts

DUBLIN
ZOO

Address Dublin Zoo, Phoenix Park, Dublin 8, Tel +353.(0)1.4748900, www.dublinzoo.ie | **Getting there** Bus routes 25, 26, 46 a, 66, 66 a, 66 b, 67, or 69; or Luas Red Line to Heuston Station, then a 15-minute walk | **Hours** Mar–Sep, daily 9.30am–6pm (last entry 5pm); Oct–Feb hours vary by month, check website. Admission: €13–€16 | **Tip** If visiting the zoo late in the day, head straight for the "African Plains Project" first. It closes half an hour earlier than the rest of the complex.

76_Oscar Wilde Sculpture
Colourful tribute, geological marvel

As befits its flamboyant subject, the sculpture of Oscar Wilde in Merrion Square is quite unlike any other piece of statuary in his native city.

First there's the way the writer is draped languidly across a boulder – a tribute to a man who once quipped: "Being natural is simply a pose." Then there are the extraordinary colours, which put all the many bronze and marble statues of surrounding Dublin in the shade.

These same colours explain why the Wilde monument is of as much interest to geologists as to fans of literature, because, in sourcing suitable materials for the work, the sculptor Danny Osborne travelled to the four corners of the earth and came back with some of its rarest stones.

The green of Wilde's smoking jacket is nephrite jade from the Yukon in Canada. The collars and cuffs are pink thulite from central Norway. The trousers, a tweedlike material called larvikite, aka blue pearl granite, with large chunks of feldspar showing through, came from a fjord near Oslo. And the shiny black shoes are a black granite material called charnokite, from India.

These appealed partly because of Wilde's known love of beautiful stones, but also for purely practical reasons. The sculpture had to retain its colours outdoors and exposed – as is inevitable in Ireland – to water. Marble is "useless" in such circumstances, according to the artist. Only the rare and ultra-hard materials chosen would do.

This also explains why, a decade after he first appeared on the boulder (35 tonnes of Irish quartz, by the way), Wilde required a head transplant. Osborne had first used ceramic for this part, but it had begun to develop cracks.

So he went travelling again, to Guatemala, and returned with a special white jade. As Wilde's permanent head, this had more than mere hardness to recommend it. In many cultures, explained the sculptor, jade is associated with immortality.

Address Opposite One Merrion Square, Dublin 2 (Wilde's childhood home),
Tel +353.(0)1.6612369, www.merrionsquare.ie | Getting there Various bus routes, including
4, 7, 44, and 66; DART rail to Westland Row, then a 5-minute walk; Luas Green Line to
St Stephen's Green; or Red Line to George's Dock, then a 10-minute walk | Tip Merrion
Square was also home (at No 82) to another famous Irish writer and Wilde's contemporary,
W B Yeats.

77 Our Lady of Dublin

A medieval statue with a talent for survival

Our Lady of Dublin is only the second most famous shrine in Whitefriar Street Church, but the statue at its centre has a long and rather colourful history. It is also unique in being the sole Irish example of a Black Madonna, a phenomenon of mysterious origin which has inspired hundreds of similar statues across Europe, some credited with miraculous powers.

The Dublin version was carved from wood, oak to be exact, probably in the late 1400s. It first stood in St Mary's Abbey, a once wealthy and powerful institution on the city's Northside. Then came the dissolution of the monasteries under Henry VIII, after which St Mary's was demoted to being a weapons store and the statue was condemned to be burned.

By some accounts, it was in fact burned, partly. But if so, it was saved from total destruction and then spent a period in hiding, disguised as a pig trough: facedown with the hollowed out back used as a feeder. After that it appears to have resurfaced at some point for use in a Jesuit chapel, before being discarded again. Then, in 1824, Father John Spratt – the same man who brought the relics of St Valentine to Dublin – spotted it in a Capel-Street shop. Ever since, it's had a permanent home in the church he built, surrounded now by opulent mosaics, in sharp contrast to the Madonna's sombre features.

She might have had an even more prominent place in the city once. In 1932, as a newly independent Irish Free State experienced a surge of piety, boosted by the millennium of St Patrick and a Eucharistic Congress in Dublin, a letter writer to the *Irish Times* called for a version of the statue to replace a certain English admiral on the top of Nelson's Pillar.

The advice was ignored and Our Lady of Dublin stayed where she was. So, for another 32 years, did Nelson, before Irish republicans adopted a more drastic approach to monument reform and blew him up.

Address Whitefriar Street Church, 56 Aungier Street, Dublin 2, www.whitefriarstreetchurch.ie | **Getting there** Bus routes 16, 65, 65b, or 122; or Luas Green Line to St Stephen's Green, then a 5-minute walk | **Hours** Mon 7.30am–6pm, Tue–Fri 7.30am–9pm, Sat 8.30am–7pm, Sun 7.30am–7pm | **Tip** If you're asking a Dubliner for directions to Aungier Street, it may be helpful to know that the name rhymes with *danger*.

78__ The Palace's Back Room

Inner sanctum of literary Dublin

There's no mistaking the literary heritage of the Palace Bar. It greets you on the way in, via four brass plaques in the pavement depicting Dublin writers. And when you pass through the pub's small front room to the even smaller back one, it's underlined by a framed cartoon on the wall, involving two of the scribes from the plaques and many more besides.

The cartoon, by New Zealander Alan Reeve, depicts the establishment on a typical night in 1940, when it hosted an assembly of Dublin's literati, including satirist Flann O'Brien and poet Patrick Kavanagh, all orbiting around their sometimes patron, sometimes employer, Bertie Smyllie, then the *Irish Times* editor.

Smyllie was one of the famed eccentrics of wartime Dublin. A rotund man, he cut a dramatic figure cycling around the city with his typewriter strung over the handlebars. Among other foibles, he was known for singing his editorials in operatic recitative and once carved his pinky fingernail into a nib for signing documents.

It may have helped the operatic performances that he and other journalists of the era tended to break their working shifts into two halves, separated by several hours in the pub. They would return to the office near midnight to resume work, sometimes fortified by carry-outs: in Smyllie's case, a naggin (quarter bottle) of brandy.

The 1940s Palace was a time and place, according to one memoirist, when "heavier or more sustained drinking may never have occurred before, or will again." But in fact, as the Four Brass-men of the Apocalypse outside could testify, epic levels of drinking were a feature of Dublin literary life in later decades too.

The regime was not without cost. At least three of the quartet in the plaques – O'Brien, Kavanagh, and Brendan Behan – had their lives shortened by drink. Only the fourth, a much-loved newspaper columnist called Con Houlihan, reached old age.

Address The Palace Bar, 21 Fleet Street, Temple Bar, Dublin 2, Tel +353.(0)1.6717388, www.thepalacebardublin.com | Getting there All City Centre bus routes; or DART rail to Tara St, then a 5-minute walk | Hours Mon–Thu 10.30am–11.30pm, Fri & Sat 10.30am–12.30am, Sun 10.30pm–11pm | Tip If you like to mix whiskey and journalism, ask for a glass of the pub's specially commissioned brand "Fourth Estate."

79___Patrick Kavanagh's Canal Bank Seats

Two commemorations for a poet who only wanted one

Realising that his adopted city might want to commemorate him posthumously, the poet Patrick Kavanagh anticipated the event in verse, prescribing "no hero-courageous tomb – just a canal bank seat for the passer by." Dublin took him at his word, but rather than a single seat, he was awarded two, one on either side of his favourite stretch of the canal.

The first, a functional wood-and-stone bench, was installed shortly after his death in 1967, complete with the text of the sonnet in which he asked for it. Beside Baggot Street Bridge, it's a pleasant place to sit, especially during what Kavanagh called "the tremendous silence of mid July." But that, by the way, was poetic licence. Baggot Street is one of central Dublin's busier thoroughfares, as is nearby Mespil Road. Silence is often scarce.

The second seat was added in the 1990s, on the opposite bank. And if you're sitting there, you'll have the poet himself – in life-size bronze effigy – for company, with his hat taking up a further space between you. Kavanagh was not always as placid as the figure depicted. Having had a love-hate relationship with his birthplace in rural Monaghan, he was never quite at peace with Dublin either, saying in later years that his move there had been "the biggest mistake of my life."

Although he traced his poetic rebirth to this part of the city, when he was recovering from cancer in the 1950s, the Grand Canal had turbulent memories too. After he fell into it one night, he claimed to have been pushed by an adversary intent on murder. He even named the would-be assassin and the motive: a newspaper article the poet had written exposing dubious business practices. Most of Kavanagh's friends doubted the story, however, believing his fall required no more sinister explanation than the evening in a pub that preceded it.

Address Mespil Road and Wilton Terrace, Dublin 2 | **Getting there** Various bus routes, including 37, 38, 38 a, 39, and 39 a | **Tip** A plaque marks Patrick Kavanagh's best-known Dublin address, 62 Pembroke Road, about a 5-minute walk from the seats.

80 __ Phil Lynott Statue

Heavy metal tribute to a rock star

Of all the Dublin statues you can stand beside, most selfie-taking tourists choose Molly Malone, the fictional fishmonger of a popular song. The cooler alternative is Phil Lynott, who, unlike Malone, really did exist, albeit not for long enough, and whose guitar-wielding likeness now stands outside one of his favourite bars, Bruxelles.

Lynott was Dublin's first rock star. Born of an Irish mother and a Guyanese father, he was also jokingly called "Ireland's first black man." And certainly, in the mono-ethnic city he grew up in during the 1960s and '70s, there were very few people with dark skin and an Afro hairstyle.

But he had both. He was also good-looking, could play a mean bass, and had a poetic turn of phrase that elevated his band, Thin Lizzy, far above the general head-banging heavy metal outfits, although they could mix it with the noisiest.

Despite, or because of, his mixed parentage, he was also fiercely proud of his Irishness. In fact, Thin Lizzy's breakthrough hit was an Irish traditional ballad, "Whiskey in the Jar," given the electric treatment. Thereafter they had a string of more conventional rock hits, including "The Boys are Back in Town" and "Dancing in the Moonlight."

Alas, like many rock stars of the era, Lynott developed a drug habit he couldn't conquer, and died way ahead of his time, in 1986, in his mid-30s. He remains a much-loved musician, celebrated annually on the anniversary of his death. Fellow guitar players have taken to inserting picks in the strings on the statue. And even the sculpture's obligatory rhyming nickname is a tribute to his popularity.

It's almost traditional now for such names to be insulting. Molly Malone's, for example, is "the Tart with the Cart," while a cane-holding James Joyce is "the Prick with the Stick." No such irreverence for Lynott, however. His statue is "the Ace with the Bass."

Address Harry Street, Dublin 2 | Getting there All City Centre bus routes; or Luas Green Line to St Stephen's Green | Tip McDaid's, just opposite the statue, is another of Dublin's famous literary bars, associated with Brendan Behan, Patrick Kavanagh, Flann O'Brien, and others.

81 The Powerscourt Centre

A once fashionable house, now a house of fashion

To call the former Powerscourt Townhouse a "shopping centre" seems a bit undignified. But the place is indeed full of shops and cafes these days. And if that's a comedown from the era when it was the third finest private home in Georgian Dublin, well, it's not such a big change of use, really.

Back in the 1700s, it was the city pad of Richard Wingfield, aka Viscount Powerscourt, and his wife Amelia. Their main abode was the magnificent Powerscourt Estate, now a five-star hotel, in Enniskerry. The townhouse – a mansion to most people – was where they entertained when parliament was in session.

It was a house for political parties, in more ways than one, and the host liked to impress. Known as the "French Earl" for the fashions he adopted after his Grand Tour of the continent, he spared no expense on the architecture and furnishings, never mind the hospitality.

So were he to see the place today, he might not be entirely displeased. The Powerscourt houses a very upmarket collection of stores, mostly devoted to fashion, as he was himself, with art, antiques, and jewellery accounting for much of the rest.

Then there are the restaurants. The biggest, Pygmalion, occupies both the central courtyard and the house's former kitchens (now a bar), and also spills over into an outdoor lounge on neighbouring Coppinger Row.

Above all, the Powerscourt still looks like a (very large) house: more than could be said in the 1970s, when it was used for offices, and the courtyard was a car park. A slight problem with its successful reinvention is that, as a listed building, it should be open to tours. And it is, up to a point. But group tours are awkward when, for example, one of the most important rooms is now a bridal salon. The current plan is to develop self-guided tours, allowing individual visitors to browse history and the shops simultaneously.

Address 59 South William Street, Dublin 2, Tel +353.(0)1.6794144, www.powerscourtcentre.ie | Getting there All City Centre bus routes; or Luas Green Line to St Stephen's Green, then a 5-minute walk | Hours Mon–Fri 10am–6pm, Thu 10am–8pm, Sat 9am–6pm, Sun noon–6pm; for guided tours contact Shireen at +353.(0)86.8065505 or shireen@gmail.com | Tip For Irish-made art, fashion, and jewellery, check out the Loft Market, a collective of independent designers on the top floor of the centre.

82__The Record Tower

Scene of a famous escape

Centuries before Andy Dufresne did it in *The Shawshank Redemption*, Red Hugh O'Donnell had broadly the same idea. The son of an Irish chieftain, he had for seven years been a prisoner in Dublin Castle, detained as a hostage to dissuade his father from rebelling against English rule. And since a previous escape attempt, he had been held in the maximum-security Record Tower: its 4.6-metre-thick walls all but impregnable.

But in January 1592, he and two fellow prisoners from the O'Neill clan made a bid for freedom via the tower's "garderobe": a polite Norman term for the toilet chute. Unlike the Shawshank escape, it was a vertical rather than horizontal journey, the trio dropping by rope into the waters below. And they too came out clean, at least metaphorically.

They were the only prisoners ever to escape from the prison, although their struggles weren't over yet. They still had to get out of English-ruled Dublin and across the Wicklow Mountains, in midwinter, with only light clothing. One of the O'Neills died from exposure. Red Hugh was luckier or more resilient, but he lost both his big toes to frostbite before freedom was assured.

Even without his toes, as the crown had feared, he proved a formidable enemy. Succeeding his father (who abdicated in his favour) as chieftain, he made common cause with Hugh O'Neill in the Nine Years War, which came close to overthrowing English rule before defeat at Kinsale in 1601. Forced to flee to Spain then, O'Donnell was still plotting a return to Ireland when he was killed by poisoning, aged 30.

Built in 1224, the Record Tower (aka the "Black," "Gunners," or "Wardrobe" tower) still stands: the only intact tower, not just of the castle, but of the old city walls, of which it formed part. In more recent times, it housed a Garda (Irish police force) museum. As of mid-2015, pending renovation, the interior was closed to visitors.

Address Lower Castle Yard, Dublin Castle, Dublin 2, Tel +353.(0)1.6458813, www.dublincastle.ie | Getting there Various bus routes including 13, 27, 40, 49, 54 a, and 747 Airlink to Dame St; or 9, 14, 15, 15 a, 15 b, 16, 65, 65b, 83, and 140 to George's St | Hours Mon–Sat 9.45am–4.45pm, Sun and bank holidays noon–4.45pm | Tip Two minutes walk from the Record Tower, on Dame Street, the City Hall has a multimedia exhibition on the history of Dublin from its Viking origins until modern times.

83__The Revenue Museum

The long and painful story of taxation

A sign in the Revenue Museum quotes the great Irish statesman Edmund Burke warning those who collect money for the public purse against expecting popularity: "To tax and to please, no more than to love and be wise, is not given to men."

The wonder, then, is that the subject of taxation was considered to have sufficient appeal among the public to deserve a museum. It is, admittedly, one of the smaller museums in Dublin, with a suitably modest location: behind a small door in the crypt of Dublin Castle's Chapel Royal. And perhaps crucially, it's also free.

From this apologetic start, its exhibits tell the interesting story of how taxes evolved from arbitrary tributes exacted by kings (of cattle, silver, and sometimes "female slaves"), to the vastly more complex system that today pays for schools and hospitals.

It reminds us that income tax, which is now matched only by death as one of life's inevitabilities, was first introduced to residents of Britain and Ireland in 1798 as a temporary measure, "to defray the recent costly American war and the French war in which we are at present involved." Indeed, 16 years later, when Napoleon was finally defeated, the government was true to its word, ending imposition. But the idea was too useful to disappear. By the mid-19th century, income tax was back, never to go away again.

The work of the revenue official was not always about collecting money. Eliminating alternatives to taxed goods, especially alcoholic ones, was a big part of the job too, especially after the creation of an Irish Border in 1922 – a boon to smugglers on either side.

The museum also details the work of the "Revenue Police" who from 1818, were dispatched to Ireland's remoter parts, where the distillation of *poitín* (a home-made and tax-free spirit) was common, and where, as an exhibit notes with Burkean understatement, "they were not received with joy."

Address Dublin Castle, Dublin 2, Tel +353.(0)1.8635601, www.revenue.ie | Getting there Various bus routes, including 13, 27, 40, 49, 54 a, and 747 Airlink to Dame St; or 9, 14, 15, 15 a, 15 b, 16, 65, and 140 to George's St | Hours Mon–Fri 10am–4pm. Admission free | Tip Don't be afraid to ask the man at the museum desk questions. He's a history enthusiast who may give you an impromptu tour.

84__The Royal Irish Academy
Not just for scholars

The Royal Irish Academy is almost entirely the preserve of scholars: few tourists venture into it. But it does have a permanent exhibition space open to all. And if you can steel yourself to penetrate the air of studiousness in its library (which you pass through en route), it's well worth a visit.

In fact, the library itself hosts small exhibitions, including a glass-covered case housing at least one exhibit from the RIA's treasury of ancient volumes at any given time. If you're really lucky, your visit might coincide with a display of the 6th-century Cathach: Ireland's oldest surviving manuscript and the second oldest Latin psalter in the world.

Tradition has it that the Cathach was the cause both of an early legal ruling on the issue of copyright and of a war. St Columba had copied it by hand from an original lent him by St Finnian, but without the latter's permission.

So, in a famous judgement, circa AD 560, the High King of Ireland declared: "To every cow her calf, to every book its copy" (a ruling all the more elegant because the books were written on vellum) – and demanded both be returned to Finnian. Columba disagreed and the row led to a battle in which 3000 men died.

Alas, because of age and fragility, the Cathach is very rarely displayed. You'll probably have to do with another of the RIA's collection of medieval books instead.

But manuscripts aside, the back room of the academy is worth seeing for its magnificent furnishings, including ornate lamps originally designed for gas, and for exhibits including Thomas Moore's harp.

Also notable are some of the benches taken – literally – from the old Irish House of Lords after the passage of the Act of Union between Great Britain and Ireland in 1800. Certain people had been members of both the parliament and the academy. When the former voted itself out of existence, they brought their seats with them.

Address 19 Dawson Street, Dublin 2, Tel +353.(0)1.6762346, www.ria.ie | **Getting there** Various bus routes, including 44, 46 a, 61, and 145; Luas Green Line to St Stephen's Green, then a 5-minute walk; or DART rail to Pearse St, then a 10-minute walk | **Hours** Mon–Thu 9.30am–5.30pm, Fri 9.30am–5pm | **Tip** The RIA is right next door to the historic St Anne's Church (Mon–Fri 10am–4pm).

85__Samuel Beckett's Foxrock
Universal characters, local footprints

You can't visit Samuel Beckett's childhood home in Foxrock, because it's a private residence. Nor can you see much of it these days, hidden as it is behind greenery on the corner of Brighton Road and Kerrymount Avenue. But you can at least walk the streets that he did. And if you stroll northwards from his home to Foxrock village on a summer's day, you can retrace the steps of his characters in at least one play: *All That Fall*, written for radio in 1956.

In general, Beckett was among the least autobiographical of writers. But as the play's chief protagonist, Maddy Rooney, sets out to meet her husband off the train as a birthday surprise, she is clearly walking along Brighton Road, while her destination, although nominally "Boghill," is Foxrock Station.

The play was provisionally titled *A Lovely Day at the Races*. And if you make the walk on one of the dates when there is a meeting in nearby Leopardstown Racecourse, you will even overhear the live commentary.

All That Fall, which takes its title from a biblical verse, is typical of Beckett's bleak outlook. When Maddy reaches the station, the train is inexplicably late. And as she and her blind husband retrace the route homeward, the mystery deepens until, finally, we learn that a child had fallen from the train en route, with fatal results. Worse, there is reason to suspect that Maddy's husband is in some way implicated, although we never find out. When pressed on the matter, the author claimed not to know the truth himself.

A winner of the Nobel Prize for Literature in 1969, Beckett spent most of his adult life in Paris, writing in French, and gradually stripping out all local detail from his writings so that his characters would be universal. Even so, a sign on a Montparnasse street named after him is very specific about the locations of his beginning and end, overlooking Dublin in favour of: "1906 Foxrock – 1989 Paris."

Address Foxrock, County Dublin | Getting there Bus routes 7 d, 46 a, 63, 84, or 84 a; or Luas Green Line to Sandyford or Carrickmines, then a 15-minute walk | Tip Look for the Beckett commemorative benches in Foxrock village, one of them bearing the title of his most famous play, *Waiting for Godot*.

86 Shaw's Birthplace

A binman's tribute to genius

His prolific writings aside, George Bernard Shaw was a lifelong socialist campaigner who co-founded the London School of Economics and is the only person ever to win both a Nobel Prize and an Oscar. So the plaque on his Dublin birthplace – "Bernard Shaw Author Of Many Plays Was Born In This House 26 July 1856" – may seem a bit on the modest side. But then again, it was composed by Shaw himself, when he was 91. And in contrast to the pale marble, it has a colourful story attached.

The impetus for the plaque came not from Shaw, but from one of his longtime admirers, a Dublin dustman named Patrick O'Reilly. O'Reilly had been born just around the corner from Shaw's home, albeit after the writer had moved to London. He collected bins in the area for 40 years and, in the late 1940s, deciding that Shaw's birthplace should be commemorated, took it upon himself to raise money for a plaque via subscriptions from his bin customers.

Then he wrote to the playwright in England proposing the following inscription – "He gave his services to his country, unlimited, unstinted, and without price" – for his approval. Not surprisingly, Shaw, who refused many honours during his lifetime, including a British knighthood, objected. "Dear Pat:" he wrote back. "Your inscription is a blazing lie. I left Dublin before I was twenty and I have devoted the remainder of my life to Labour and International Socialism and for all you know I may be hanged yet." He then suggested the alternative wording, and the wreath of shamrock that circles the plaque.

One of Shaw's most famous characters, Eliza Doolittle, was the daughter of a dustman. She featured in the 1913 play *Pygmalion*, which was among the many works that earned the author his Nobel Prize for Literature in 1925. He jointly won his Oscar for the 1938 film adaptation of the play, later remade as *My Fair Lady*.

87__The Sick & Indigent Roomkeepers Society

A sign of times past

The Sick and Indigent Roomkeepers Society no longer operates out of the handsome building at No 2 Palace Street. It did for nearly 140 years, however, and left a deep impression. Now and for the foreseeable future, the unusual name remains cut heavily into the building's stonework, making it one of Dublin's favourite "ghost" signs.

Founded in 1790, and still in business, the society is the city's oldest surviving charity. But its name probably requires explanation for a modern audience. Many visitors may need to Google even the word *indigent* (it means poor). And as for *roomkeepers*, which might seem to describe people in the hotel industry, it used to mean simply those who occupied rooms, often alone and in bad circumstances.

The charity was first based across the river in St Michan's parish, an impoverished area where the founders were moved by the plight of "many poor creatures who were unable to dig and ashamed to beg … and were often found dead in the sequestered garrets and cellars to which they had silently returned." So the charity had a broad remit then and has an even broader one now, helping the city's poor in general. Its former home is a private residence these days and therefore, apart from being a popular photo opportunity, inaccessible.

But Palace Street has several other points of interest for visitors. It leads into Dublin Castle. It's home to the French restaurant, Chez Max, a piece of transplanted Paris. And with a grand total of two front doors, Palace Street also claims to be the city's shortest.

Less happily, No 2 is now flanked by a small office block erected on the adjoining square in 2006 and already one of Dublin's least liked buildings. Too unpopular even for an insulting nickname, it is typically referred to as "that thing on Dame Street."

Address 2 Palace Street, Dublin 2, www.roomkeepers.com | Getting there Various bus routes, including 13, 16, 40, and 123 | Tip Palace Street is only a 2-minute walk from another famous Dublin landmark – the neon "Why Go Bald?" sign – on Dame Lane.

88_ Silicon Docks
New technology reviving old Dublin

Where California has Silicon Valley, Dublin has the Silicon Docks: a hub of high-tech companies, including Google, Facebook, Twitter, and LinkedIn, all of which have located European headquarters in the Irish capital. It gets the second half of its name from Grand Canal Dock, where the first and biggest concentration of firms is based. But later arrivals have spread well beyond that area, and the name is now more notional than geographic.

The phenomenon began in the early years of the century, when Ireland's Industrial Development Authority aggressively targeted U.S. tech companies. The big catch was Google, which having agreed to open a Dublin HQ, encouraged others to follow. But Google expanded fastest and farthest. By 2015, between staff and contract workers, the company claimed to employ more than 5000 people in the city. And as well as being big, its workforce is extraordinarily diverse, with an estimated 70 nationalities and almost as many languages.

The tech companies point to a variety of reasons that make Dublin attractive, including the fact that Ireland has the youngest population in Europe, with high education levels. But very low corporate tax is a big factor too, to the chagrin of larger EU economies.

In any case, the phenomenon has revived the once dying docklands. More generally, since the vast majority of workers are 20- and 30-somethings, it adds to the youthful buzz of what is now a vibrant, cosmopolitan city.

Long remote from Europe's major centres of population, Dublin has revelled in communications technology. Among the spin-offs of the Silicon Docks phenomenon was the Web Summit, held annually here for five years until 2015, when it announced a move to Lisbon. The Dublin summit attracted 30,000 networking techies at its height, and the social programme was a key to its success. Some of the best-attended events were the nightly pub crawls.

Address Google's Dublin headquarters, Barrow Street, Dublin 4; other companies in the area include Facebook and Airbnb | **Getting there** DART rail to Barrow St **Hours** Not open to the public; viewable from the outside | **Tip** Some of the workplaces welcome the general public during the annual Open House weekend in October (www.openhousedublin.ie).

89__Smithfield Square

Where Cold War Berlin met Dublin

Although mostly set in communist East Germany, the classic espionage movie *The Spy Who Came in from the Cold* (1965) was partly shot in Dublin. Cobblestoned Smithfield Square provided the location of the film's Checkpoint Charlie, the infamous crossing point between East and West Berlin. And it's said that as a stand-in for that wintry city, then in the grip of the Cold War, 1960s Dublin was more convincing than the real thing.

Half a century later, Smithfield is still a sort of crossing point between two halves of a city, in this case Dublin old and new. For years now there have been attempts to upgrade the square (which is actually a long rectangle), turning it into a local version of Rome's cafe-lined Piazza Navona, to which it has similar proportions.

This plan came into conflict, however, with Smithfield's traditional role as a marketplace, including its hosting of a monthly horse fair, held here for centuries. For that and other reasons, the gentrification has been a mixed success. The horse fair, under pressure anyway because of complaints about animal cruelty and occasional rowdiness, has now been reduced to a biannual affair, and even then is much scaled back from its heyday.

But the attempted architectural improvements have also been uneven. They include a gigantic set of 12 lampposts topped by (rarely lit) gas burners on one flank. And the buildings are lopsided too. The south and west of the square is dominated by large, modern apartment blocks, while a number of small 1980s council houses, and the popular Cobblestone Pub, cling to the northeast corner.

The undoubted successes of the redevelopment, so far, include the Light House. A multi-screen art-house cinema, it also boasts a cafe, bar, and recreation space, complete with that hipster essential: table tennis. Perhaps significantly, in Cold War terms it's on the square's Western side.

Address Smithfield, Dublin 7; Light House Cinema, Tel +353.(0)1.8728006, www.lighthousecinema.ie | Getting there Various bus routes, including 25, 25 a, 25 b, 66, 66 a, 66 b, and 67; or Luas Red Line to Smithfield stop | Tip Just off Smithfield, on Bow Street, is the old Jameson Distillery, which offers daily tours, tastings, and a restaurant.

90_ Smock Alley Theatre

Dublin's oldest new theatre

Smock Alley is the oldest theatre in Dublin, but it's also one of the newest. This paradox is explained by a theatrical history in two acts, divided by a very long interval: more than 200 years long, in fact.

It was partly a drinks interval. For years after its closure in 1787, it served as a whiskey warehouse. Then it became a church, and even that was theatrical. When it opened in 1811, marking the retreat of the Penal Laws (although Catholic Emancipation was still some years away), it was the first Catholic church to ring its bells in the city since the Reformation.

But back to its earlier spell as a theatre, which began in 1662. In the century that followed, it introduced some famous plays to the world, including Goldsmith's *She Stoops to Conquer* and Richard Brinsley Sheridan's *The Rivals* and *The School for Scandal*. This despite structural problems relating to its riverside location on reclaimed land, which meant that the action was not always confined to the stage. On one infamous occasion in 1670, during a Ben Jonson play, the upper gallery collapsed onto the middle one, causing that in turn to crash down onto ground-floor seats, killing a "poor girlie."

There was another collapse in 1735. And yet, nearly three centuries later, when the by now closed church on the site was excavated by archaeologists, it was discovered that the old theatre had not been demolished, as long believed, but that the 1662 foundations and much of the post-1735 rebuild remained.

So after major renovation, the theatre reopened on its original site, with three separate performance spaces and a banquet hall. It held on to some of the church features, including ornate ceiling plaster and stained glass windows. But it retains much of its earlier form, making it, as the Smock Alley website claims, "one of the most important sites in European theatre history."

Address 6–7 Exchange Street, Dublin 2, Tel +353.(0)1.6770014, www.smockalley.com |
Getting there Various bus routes, including 37, 39, 39 a, 51 d, 69, 83, and 145 to Wood
Quay; or Luas Red Line to Jervis or Four Courts, then a 5-minute walk. | Hours Box
office: Mon–Sat 10am–6pm, Sun (performance days only) noon–8pm | Tip The
"Freedom Bell" on the roof of the theatre – said to have been cracked when rung in
violation of the Penal Laws in 1811 – received a Department of Tourism grant for
restoration in 2014.

91_ St Audoen's Anglican Church

An ancient church with a lucky charm

Among the ancient artefacts in St Audoen's is one that has become known as the "lucky stone." In fact, it's a 9th-century gravestone and, as such, indicates that the current church, built by Dublin's Norman invaders in 1190, is on the site of an even older one. But the stone's association with good fortune is old too, going back to at least the 13th century.

It was considered sufficiently auspicious that, in 1308, when the city's first public water cistern was erected in nearby Cornmarket, the stone was taken from the church and placed alongside. Drinking water was indeed a risky activity then: beer was often safer. So the stone's supposed powers reinforced the faith of those partaking.

But its reputation extended well beyond water purification. Local businessmen believed that touching it daily was a prerequisite for success. And for pilgrims setting out on the Camino de Santiago, the lucky stone was a compulsory stop, ensuring safe passage.

Of course, with such powers, it was much coveted. But part of its supernatural reputation was an ability to find its way back to St Audoen's on the several occasions it went missing. Once, in 1826, it was taken by a group of country people, who were transporting it out of Dublin when, it is said, the stone grew heavier and heavier until it collapsed the cart and the thieves had to abandon it. On that or another occasion, it was also reported to have taken on human characteristics. Found by stonemasons who attempted to break it, it moaned and groaned until they stopped.

But remarkable as it might be, the lucky stone is only one of many reasons why St Audoen's is worth a visit. It's Dublin's oldest medieval parish church still in use. It represents at least 1000 years of history on what used to be the city's main street.

Address 14 High Street, Dublin 8, Tel +353.(0)1.6770088, www.cja.dublin.anglican.org |
Getting there Bus routes 13, 40, and 123 | Hours 25 Apr–23 Oct, daily 9.30am–5.30pm;
last admission: 4.45pm | Tip Audoen is a Norman name, pronounced "Aud-owen."
But if asking directions, be aware that the local pronunciation of the church is more
like "St Audience."

92 St Enda's School

A nursery for rebels

Now the Pearse Museum, St Enda's School started out as a short-lived experiment in the educational ideas of Patrick Pearse. The son of an English stonemason who moved to Dublin, Pearse grew up to be both a teacher and a fervent Irish nationalist. His school at Rathfarnham was dedicated not just to the academic development of children, it was also intended to prepare them for revolution.

Along with his brother Willie, Pearse created St Enda's as a place where centuries of Anglicisation in Ireland would be reversed. Students were taught their native language and culture. They played the ancient Gaelic game of hurling, in kilts. They acted out plays and pageants dressed as mythological heroes.

The school had progressive ideas about education in general. Children were encouraged to spend time outdoors, working in the garden and communing with nature. Teaching was child-centred, aiming to unleash each individual's potential. But outside of school, Pearse was also a leader of the militant Irish Republican Brotherhood, and he had very definite ideas about his own life's purpose.

On Easter Monday 1916, he read the Proclamation of the Irish Republic on the steps of the General Post Office in Dublin, then joined a weeklong armed rebellion inside that was eventually crushed by the British authorities. Both Pearse brothers were among 16 rebel leaders subsequently executed for their part in the Rising. Patrick Pearse is said to have whistled as he went to face the firing squad.

In all, five of those executed had taught at St Enda's. More than 30 of the GPO garrison had spent time in Pearse's school. After his death, the institution struggled on until the 1930s, before closing in what was now an independent Ireland. Gifted to the state in 1968, it was subsequently reopened as a museum dedicated to the Pearse brothers and the history of the school.

Address The Pearse Museum, St Enda's Park, Grange Road, Rathfarnham, Dublin 16, Tel. +353.(0)1.4934208, www.heritageireland.ie/en/pearsemuseum | **Getting there** Bus route 16 to Grange Rd, stopping at St Enda's Park | **Hours** Mar–Oct, daily 9.30am–5.30pm; Nov–Jan, daily 9.30am–4pm; Feb, daily 9.30am–5pm | **Tip** Laid out in the 18th century, the grounds of what is now the museum contain a collection of follies inspired by ancient Ireland, including a hermit's cave, a dolmen, and an ogham stone.

93__St Mary's Chapel of Ease
A church with a dark reputation

You can't get into the "Black Church" – officially St Mary's Chapel of Ease – anymore, unless you have an appointment with one of the businesses that now occupy its deconsecrated interior.

Failing that, you won't be able to appreciate such dramatic features as the parabolic arch by which its walls curve inwards to become the roof. But the building's folklorish infamy had less to do with parabolic spaces than diabolic ones. And you can still test out that reputation, if so inclined.

In a tradition inspired by its dark and ominous appearance, it used to be said that if you circled the church three times in an anti-clockwise direction, the devil would appear and steal your soul. In some versions, you had to run, and it had to be at midnight. Other terms and conditions may have applied, depending on the teller.

And it's unclear if there were ever any recorded appearances by the evil one. But the legend was strong enough to hover over the 1962 autobiography of Dublin poet Austin Clarke. He grew up nearby and, taking no chances even with a book title, called his memoir *Twice Round the Black Church*.

Sixty years earlier, almost inevitably, the building also merited mention in James Joyce's *Ulysses*, during a dream sequence in which the main protagonist finds himself in court, accused of various sins, including entry into a "clandestine marriage with at least one woman in the shadow of the Black Church." So its occult fame was not confined to the circling myth.

The building was deconsecrated in the 1960s, and its supernatural associations, good and bad, have faded since. The nearest connection with evil in modern times is when it housed Dublin Corporation's traffic wardens. And although the outer walls are as black as ever, there is still a fully natural explanation: the architect's use of a type of limestone known as calp, which turns dark in the rain.

Address St Mary's Place, Broadstone, Dublin 7 | Getting there Various bus routes, including 1, 16, 38, 38 a, 38 b, 40 d, and 122 | Tip In contrast with the church's dark reputation, note the name of the street opposite its northeast corner: Paradise Place.

94_ St Michan's Church

Shaking hands with history

Visitors to St Michan's Church used to be invited to shake hands with one of the older members of its congregation, known as the crusader. Unfortunately, given his age – about 800 years – he was in rather delicate condition. So when one of his fingers was damaged at some point, the handshaking stopped. Now, the most you can do is touch his hand, which is still said to bring good luck.

Like other residents of the St Michan's Crypt, the "crusader" is a mummified skeleton: his bones covered by a thin layer of desiccated skin and centuries of dust. Preserved by the dry air and constant temperatures of the crypt, he shares his vault with several other exposed mummies whose coffins have crumbled. They include the "thief," so named because one of his hands was chopped off, although if he really was a thief, he must have repented, or he would never have earned such an honoured resting place.

All bodies in St Michan's crypt are presumed mummified, but in most other vaults the coffins remain intact, their contents untouched and untouchable. In some cases, they're piled on top of one another. But not the unfortunate Sheares Brothers, John and Henry, who have a tomb to themselves, where they lie side by side. Inspired by the French Revolution, they were centrally involved in Ireland's republican insurrection of 1798. Their punishment was to be "hung, drawn, and quartered" (partial hanging, followed by disembowelment while alive, then decapitation, and the quartering of the body). Alongside their coffins is the death mask of another patriot, Wolfe Tone, who escaped a similar fate by taking his own life in prison.

It's speculated that the atmospheric grounds of St Michan's may have had a formative effect on one young Dubliner who used to visit there in the late 19th century. His name was Bram Stoker, and the name of his most famous character is often said to be a contraction of the Irish words for "bad blood": *droch-fhola*, or Dracula, for short.

Address Church Street, Dublin 7, Tel +353.(0)1.8724154, www.stmichans.com | Getting there Bus route 83; or Luas Red Line to Four Courts or Smithfield stops, then a 2-minute walk | Hours 16 Mar–1 Nov, Mon–Fri 10am–12.45pm and 2pm–4.45pm, Sat 10am–4pm | Tip In the church itself, look for the beautiful wood carving in the front of the pipe organ, depicting 17 instruments and dating from 1724.

95__St Nicholas of Myra Church

Scene of a Catholic comeback

On the margins of an old map in the porch of St Nicholas' Church is an amusing, if racist, 12th-century cartoon. Under the caption "Irishmen demonstrate the axe," it features a crudely drawn tree and two even cruder men with hatchets. They're supposed to be chopping down the tree, clearly, but the joke is that one of the pair has instead planted his axe in the other man's skull.

The picture was among the illustrations in a book about Ireland published in 1188 by Giraldus Cambrensis, an Anglo-Norman historian. He took a dim view of the Irish, generally. But that may have been part of his brief, because as the official chronicler of the Norman invasion, he had a vested interest in portraying the natives as a people in dire need of civilising. Thus what had not long before been considered an island of saints and scholars was recast as the home of savages, incapable of self-improvement. And his writings on the subject set the tone of Anglo-Irish relations for centuries, until later generations of historians took him to task. By then the reformation had driven another wedge between the Irish, who remained predominantly Catholic, and their Protestant English rulers. There followed centuries of religious discrimination, through the Penal Laws.

Hence the significance of St Nicholas', which was built in 1829: the year when, in the final unraveling of those laws, Catholics were granted the vote. St Nicholas' was among a wave of churches to be built across Ireland in subsequent decades, and it's a rather beautiful one, with exquisite ceiling decoration and a marble altar.

But it was also a tentative first step towards religious expression, because even in 1829, it wasn't the done thing for Catholic churches to be too prominent. Hence the discreet location of St Nicholas': set as far back from the main local thoroughfare as the site allowed.

Address Francis Street, Dublin 8, Tel +353.(0)1.5611390, www.francisstreetparish.ie | Getting there Various bus routes, including 13, 40, 49, 51 a, 77, 123, and 150 | Hours Daily 9.30am – noon | Tip Francis Street is also synonymous with the antiques business, having the greatest concentration of such shops in Dublin.

96__ St Patrick's Tower
A windmill at rest

Ask most Dubliners where St Patrick's Tower is and you'll get blank looks, even though it's one of the city's most conspicuous landmarks. Only if you mention that it's an old windmill might they direct you to the thing on Thomas Street, long without sails or function and now standing idly in the car park of an office block.

As for the name, even those who pass it every day may be at a loss to explain what St Patrick has to do with the tower. But if you gaze up at the top of its 40-metre height, he's there all right: in small, less-than-life-size effigy, like a weather vane.

The structure is what's known as a "smock" windmill, after its distinctive top, which used to bear sails and could turn 360 degrees to catch the breeze. It's said to be the tallest such tower in Europe.

In any case, when it was built in 1757, the proprietors saw fit to invoke the national saint's blessing on the enterprise. Which was in dubious taste, really, because their business was whiskey: long considered the curse of the Irish, especially by the clergy. Helped by local demand, George Roe Distillers grew to become the world's biggest whiskey manufacturer. At the company's height, it occupied a 17-acre site and exported millions of bottles annually, all under the supervision of the tiny figure with his cross and mitre.

Then Roe's, and the Irish whiskey industry in general, went into sharp decline. A (clerical-led) temperance movement, changing tastes, the First World War, and U.S. Prohibition all contributed to the slide. Today, hardly anyone in Dublin remembers Roe's.

As he looks down on the decommissioned windmill, however, the saint is not quite high and dry. The winds of change may have seen off the unholy spirit, but now, instead, the Apostle of Ireland presides over a vast brewery that occupies the entire former Roe's site and several city blocks besides, and is known by the name of Guinness.

Address The Digital Hub car park, Thomas Street, Dublin 8, Tel +353.(0)1.4806200 | Getting there Bus routes 13, 40, or 123 | Hours Not open to the public; viewable from the outside | Tip Look for the old pear tree at the tower's base. One of Ireland's heritage trees, it's believed to date from the middle of the 19th century.

97 St Valentine's Relics

A shrine for young lovers

"The course of true love never did run smooth," as Shakespeare said, and the path by which the patron saint of love ended up in Dublin is complicated too. He was a Roman by birth, or maybe even two Romans whose cults became intertwined. In any case, his martyrdom (by beheading, at the order of Emperor Claudius) is usually dated to around AD 269.

Fast-forward a millennium and a half, to the 1830s, when an Irish Carmelite priest, Father John Spratt, visited the Eternal City. His preaching there impressed the Roman Catholic elite, including Pope Gregory XVI, who was also aware of Spratt's work among Dublin's poor. Learning that the priest had built a new church back home, the Pope made him a prestigious present: St Valentine's remains (minus the head, which stayed in Rome). These were enshrined with great ceremony in Dublin in 1836.

Several other places throughout Europe claim to have parts of St Valentine, and probably do, since it wasn't unusual once for sacred relics to be divided. But the Dublin shrine is vouched for by the Vatican and much venerated, especially on 14 February, when it's the focus of an annual blessing of the rings for couples about to wed.

As with all the facts of his life, it's not clear why Valentine became the patron of love in particular. One legend is that he used to marry young couples in secret, thereby excusing the husbands from military duty, much to the emperor's annoyance. Another is that, when imprisoned for refusing to make sacrifices to pagan gods, he prayed for the jailer's daughter, who was blind, to regain her sight, and she did. Then, before his execution, he left her a letter signed "your Valentine."

In any case, his cult is still alive in Dublin. The shrine includes a book wherein visitors can write out requests to the saint. Many do, and their petitions range from the general to the very particular, e.g.: "Please help my sister find a good husband."

Address 56 Aungier Street, Dublin 2, Tel +353.(0)1.4758821, www.whitefriarstreetchurch.ie | **Getting there** Bus routes 16, 65, 65 b, or 122 to Aungier St; or Luas Green Line to St Stephen's Green, then a 10-minute walk | **Hours** Mon & Wed–Sat 7.30am–6pm, Tue 7.30am–9pm Sat 8.30am–7pm, Sun 7.30am–7pm | **Tip** Look out for the shrine of the church's lesser-known Italian saint, Albert of Sicily, and his miraculous "St Albert's water."

ST.VALENTINE.....*listen*

98 St Werburgh's Church
Ringing bells and fighting fires

A fascinating sign in St Werburgh's Church advertises a list of religious services offered in the year 1728, along with a breakdown of prices. There are two rates for everything: one for parishioners, and another – more expensive – for "foreigners," who could expect to pay extra for a wedding, burial, or even for a "muffled" ringing of church bells. The latter was a luxury service, wherein bell-clappers were covered with leather to produce a softer, subdued sound in tribute to a departed soul. While it cost a hefty £1.1s for a parishioner, it was six shillings more for outsiders.

But religious services were not the only ones offered by St Werburgh's, as a pair of unusual exhibits in the atrium attest. It used to be the case that churches were also responsible for firefighting in their parishes, a duty that became all the more pressing after the Great Fire of London in 1666.

Fearing a similar disaster in Dublin, St Werburgh's decided to upgrade its service with that era's cutting-edge technology, which happened to be French. But rather than import this at great expense, the canny church sent its parish engineer to France where, posing as a buyer, he took detailed notes, then came back and built the machines himself.

Although still an impressive building, St Werburgh's has come down in the world since its 18th-century heyday. It used to have a tower and spire soaring 50 metres above street level. But this, among other things, gave it a view into the adjacent Dublin Castle, the centre of English rule. And after the republican uprisings of 1798 and 1803, such a view (and its accompanying opportunities for a marksman) became a problem. The authorities affected concern about structural weaknesses in the tower supporting the spire, and a number of well-chosen architects agreed. The spire was removed in 1810. The tower followed some years later.

Address Werburgh Street, Dublin 8, Tel +353.(0)1.4783710 | Getting there Bus routes 50, 50a, 54, 54a, and 56a | Hours The building is usually closed, but visits may be arranged by phone | Tip The church still holds two services a month, on the first and third Sundays at 10am.

99__Sunlight Chambers

A monument to soap

The Irish capital has long been known, more or less affectionately, as "dear old dirty Dublin." But however much it deserves that description today, it was certainly a much dirtier place in the 19th century. By the late 1800s, however, sanitation services began to improve dramatically. So when establishing a new Dublin headquarters in 1899, the Liverpool detergent company Lever Brothers decided that the building itself should promote the concept of cleanliness.

The result was a series of friezes, wrapped around three sides of "Sunlight Chambers," depicting the history of hygiene. The sculpted terra-cotta panels, painted in vibrant colours, showed scenes from the making and use of soap products, and they soon became a much-loved city landmark.

Not everyone liked them at first. Early reviews included one from an Irish construction magazine that claimed the new addition was "the ugliest building in Dublin," calling it both "pretentious and mean." And the Florentine architecture was certainly unusual in a predominantly Georgian city. But perhaps it was equally relevant to the criticisms that the design team was English. In any case, Sunlight Chambers survived to become a local favourite, outliving Lever Brothers and a succession of other tenants since, including the Revenue Commissioners.

By the end of the 20th century, the building had itself grown rather grimy from years of exposure to smog and traffic emissions. But in 1999 it was restored to full glory, with the panels repainted and reglazed, although for the exterior walls, the restorers decided against the original white and opted for a more practical yellow.

The building now houses a solicitor's practice and as such is not open to the general public. But it doesn't really matter, because apart from an ornamental staircase, all the main points of interest are on the outside.

Address Corner of Parliament Street and Essex Quay, Dublin 2 | Getting there Bus routes 37, 39, 39 a, 69, 70, 79 a, 83, 83 a, or 145; or Luas Red Line to Four Courts or Jervis, then a 5-minute walk | Hours Not open to the public; viewable from the outside | Tip A minute's walk from Sunlight Chambers along Parliament Street is Thomas Read's Cutlers, Dublin's oldest shop. Established in 1670, it originally sold swords, among other goods. Alas, it has been closed since 1997 and, as of 2015, is in very poor condition.

100__ Sweny's Chemist
Cleaning up after James Joyce

When it was first published in the 1920s, James Joyce's *Ulysses* was considered a very "dirty" book, especially by those who hadn't read it. Its frankness about sex and other bodily functions earned a ban in Britain and it was prosecuted for indecency in the U.S. So it's rather apt that the novel is now commemorated annually by, among other things, the purchase of soap.

Although modelled on Homer's *Odyssey*, *Ulysses* concerns the more prosaic events of a day in the life of Dublin: 16 June 1904. In the real world, this was the date Joyce first went out with his future wife, Nora Barnacle. But the book's hero is the fictional Leopold Bloom, whose wanderings around the city are now reenacted every 16 June – "Bloomsday" – by enthusiasts.

One of the routine errands he performs in the novel is collecting a prescription from Sweny's Chemists on Lincoln Place. While there, he buys a bar of lemon soap, raising it to his nose and smelling its "sweet lemony wax" as he pays. This has become one of the most popular parts of the reenactment: all the more so because it doesn't require any familiarity with the text. In fact, *Ulysses* remains a book much more talked about than read. It's still considered too difficult for all but the most committed bookworms. And one of the attractions of Bloomsday is that you can hear lots of other people, often actors, reciting parts of it aloud for you. Hardened Joyceans, however, now gather in the tiny chemist's shop not just on 16 June but on most days throughout the year for group readings, in multiple languages.

Sweny's has long since ceased to be a working pharmacy. But on special occasions, visitors sometimes medicate themselves with liquid prescriptions carried across the road from Kennedy's Pub. Joyce aside, the shop also serves as a tiny museum to Dublin as it was in 1904. As well as soap, the volunteers who staff it sell second-hand books, postcards, and other souvenirs.

Address 1 Lincoln Place, Dublin 2, Tel +353.87.7132157, www.sweny.ie | Getting there Various bus routes to Clare St and Westland Row, including 4, 7, 44, and 66; or DART rail to Pearse St Station, then a 2-minute walk | Hours Mon–Sat 11am–5pm, or by arrangement | Tip High on a gable wall near Sweny's, look out for the sign advertising the former "Finn's Hotel," now otherwise vanished, where Nora Barnacle worked as a chambermaid.

101 The Táin Mosaic

An epic tale, told in tiles

On a wall beside the entrance to an underground car park in central Dublin is a mosaic mural depicting scenes from an Irish mythological saga. Set in the 1st century, the *Táin Bó Cuailnge* has been described as "Ireland's Iliad," although the transcriber of the 12th-century *Book of Leinster*, which includes a version of the epic, saw fit to issue a disclaimer.

"I who have copied down this story, or more accurately fantasy, do not credit the details of the story of fantasy," he wrote. "Some things in it are devilish lies, or some poetical figments. Some seem possible and others not. Some are for the enjoyment of idiots."

That colophon used to be displayed alongside the mural. Now it's gone, and there's nothing else to explain the work to those who don't know what it is, not even a mention of the artist's name (Desmond Kinney, who died in 2014) or the date of completion (1974).

What remains, for now, is the mosaic, which features highlights of the conflict that resulted when Queen Maeve of Connacht sent her armies into Ulster on a mission to steal the famed "Brown Bull of Cooley."

After much slaughter, the battle culminated in single-combat between the teenage champion of Ulster, Cúchulainn, and his childhood friend and foster brother, Ferdia, Maeve's greatest soldier. They fought for three days, knocking lumps out of each other (in the poetic original, even their lesser wounds are big enough for birds to fly through), before Cúchulainn deployed his semi-magical weapon, a foot-thrown spear called the Gae Bolga, and with a heavy heart, killed his friend.

The mural was commissioned by the builders of the Setanta Centre ("Setanta" was Cúchulainn's boyhood name), whose tenants included a branch of the Irish civil service. But the complex has changed ownership at least once in the intervening years, and in the process, the mural appears to have become an orphan.

Address Setanta Centre, Nassau Street, Dublin 2 | Getting there Various bus routes including 4, 7, 8, 15 a, 15 b, 46 a, 116, and 145; DART rail to Pearse St, then a 5-minute walk; or Luas Green Line to St Stephen's Green, then a 5-minute walk | Hours Always viewable | Tip For an entertaining account of the Táin wall, see the website of "bardic storyteller" Richard Marsh at www.mazgeenlegendary.wordpress.com and click on *Setanta Wall*.

102 — Thomas Heazle Parke Statue

Lessons in the struggle for survival

Guarding the entrance to the Natural History Museum is the rifle-wielding statue of Thomas Heazle Parke: a man who, despite the gun, was better known for saving lives than taking them. He was a soldier (and naturalist), but also a surgeon – chief surgeon, in fact – on one of the 19th century's last major expeditions into the African interior. Hence the dramatic scene depicted in a relief sculpture under the statue, which shows him sucking poison from the chest of a fellow officer who had been hit by an arrow.

Parke saved that man's life and many others. But the supposedly humanitarian mission was still a bit of a disaster, not least because of shortage of food. In one of the lighter passages of his diaries, reversing the usual story of colonial exploitation, he describes hard-headed negotiations with local tribal chiefs who demand various items from the Europeans in return for chickens and other supplies: "Their object in giving us little or no food is to starve us into parting with our rifles and ammunition: which we are determined not to do – at least until all our own belongings go first." This might explain why the bronze version of Parke is holding tight to his gun, although it didn't save him from his ultimate nemesis. Having survived the expedition, he died a few years later, aged 35, possibly from the effects of a tapeworm.

As with the explorers and chiefs, struggles for food are of course a running theme in the building behind Parke, and probably explain the extinction of the museum's prize exhibit: the giant Irish deer, two examples of which greet you inside the entrance. The largest deer species ever, they had enormous antlers, requiring high levels of certain nutrients, including calcium. One theory is that it was the catastrophic depletion of their food supply during the last ice age that led to their disappearance, some 10,000 years ago.

Address Natural History Museum, Merrion Street, Dublin 2, Tel +353.(0)1.6777444, www.musum.ie | Getting there Various bus routes to Merrion Square, including 4, 7, 25, 25a, 25b, 26, and 44; Luas Green Line to St Stephen's Green, then an 8-minute walk; or DART rail to Pearse Station, then an 8-minute walk | Hours Tue–Sat 10am–5pm, Sun 2pm–5pm | Tip Look for the museum's 19th-century polar bear, complete with the bullet hole that killed him.

103___Tully Church & High Crosses

Ancient ruins in a leafy suburb

Follow the Brennanstown Road out of Cabinteely in suburban southeast Dublin, then take a left for Lehaunstown, and in less than a kilometre you will think you're in deepest rural Ireland. As the narrow boreen twists and turns before you through green fields, it's hard to believe you're surrounded by urban sprawl. Then the illusion is broken by the appearance ahead of the M50, the city's orbital motorway, and you realise you haven't left Dublin at all.

Yet here, barely a mile from Cabinteely, is a remarkable trio of medieval Christian ruins, dating back to a time when the city barely existed. You first meet a Celtic cross, raised onto a platform in the 1800s during roadworks, but otherwise a relic from the 12th century. Farther on are the picturesque remains of Tully Church, also 12th century but probably built on the site of a structure several hundred years older. This was still a functioning church as late as 1615, although by 1630, storms were reported to have damaged it badly.

For the third part of the ensemble – a very weather-beaten cross with a missing arm and traces of a carved figure on one side – you have to search harder. It's in the middle of an open field opposite the church, accessible by a gap in the hedge. From here, thanks to the fine views, you can sense the origins of the name "Tully" – a corruption of an Irish word for "mound" or "hill" – and why the location recommended itself as an ecclesiastical site.

Retracing your journey, if you go left instead of right at Brennanstown Road, you will soon be in Foxrock, one of Dublin's most exclusive suburbs. There you can see Tullow Church, the modern successor to the ruined one. A plainer structure, it has at least one claim to fame: among its former parishioners was the Nobel-winning writer Samuel Beckett.

Address Lehaunstown (also spelt Laughanstown), Cabinteely, County Dublin,
Tel +353.(0)1.2893154 (Tullow Church), www.tullow.dublin.anglican.org | **Getting there**
Bus routes 84, 84 a, or 145 to Cabinteely, then a 15-minute walk; or Luas Green Line
to Lehaunstown | Tip For an unusual view of the Tully High Cross, see the cover of the
1973 album *Happy to Meet, Sorry to Part* by the Celtic rock band Horslips.

104__ Vico Road, Killiney
The Bay of Naples, Irish-style

As you head south from Dalkey village, you may notice a dramatic change in the place names: one suggesting that the great body of water off to your left is not the Irish Sea, as you thought, but the Tyrrhenian.

Suddenly, the roads all seem to be called after places in Italy: Sorrento, Vico, Nerano. So are the houses: Amalfi, Casini, San Elmo. And the reason may become apparent as you climb Vico Road, with the beach and railway line far below you.

No, it's not because there are high numbers of Italian immigrants in these parts. It's because Dubliners maintain the fond belief that, in terms of scenery, this is the Irish equivalent of the Bay of Naples.

In a mixing of geographic metaphors, the elevated roads around this area are also sometimes called the Hollywood Hills of Dublin, since this is where many of the local rich and famous live.

But getting back to Italy, the view of the bay does certainly have something in common with Sorrento or Amalfi, although Dalkey Island is hardly the Isle of Capri, and at 170 metres, Killiney Hill is a bit too modest (and non-volcanic) to be mistaken for Mount Vesuvius. In fact the only thing that has erupted around here in recent times is the cost of property. And with some of the most fiercely coveted real estate in Ireland, the area has seen some very high-profile legal disputes of late.

Still, some of the best parts are in public ownership, including Killiney Hill Park. That used to be private too, but in 1887 it was bought for the people of Dublin as a jubilee gift to mark Queen Victoria's 50th year on the throne.

These days, the trek up to its crowning obelisk (built in 1742 as an employment-creating scheme during a harsh winter) is popular with those in search of exercise as well as views. And if that's not steep enough, you can also have a go at the cliff walls of Dalkey Quarry, now abandoned but a magnet for rock climbers.

Address Vico Road, Killiney, County Dublin | **Getting there** Bus route 8 from Dublin City Centre, or 59 from Dún Laoghaire; or DART rail to Dalkey Station, then a 15-minute walk. There are two pedestrian routes to Killiney Park from Vico Rd | **Tip** Visit the uninhabited Dalkey Island, just 300 metres off the coast, by rowboat (see kentheferryman.com for details). Packed picnics can be arranged.

105__ Vonolel's Grave

The last resting place of a four-legged war hero

Most of the old soldiers buried in the Royal Hospital Kilmainham (RHK) had only two legs. Indeed some had fewer than two as a result of services to king and country. But at least one of them had four.

His name was Vonolel and he was a horse: a handsome white Arabian stallion, to be exact. He had served in the Afghan campaigns of the 1880s. And for his heroics, Queen Victoria awarded him several medals, along with the honour of leading her jubilee procession through London. He also happened to be owned by Rudyard Kipling's favourite general, the Anglo-Irish Lord Roberts, who became the army's Commander in Chief.

So when this very well-connected animal died at the RHK, he was buried with full honours, or at least a handsome headstone (complete with a poem expressing his owner's hope that they will meet again in Heaven), in an exclusive plot in the walled gardens.

After 250 years in military service, the hospital fell derelict after Irish independence, but has since then been restored and reinvented as the Irish Museum of Modern Art. Today, the main building houses abstract exhibits, while the old soldiers are confined to cemeteries: officers in one, privates in another, reflecting the class-consciousness of former times.

Vonolel, by the way, was not the only four-legged hero of the Afghan wars. A dog called Bobby, described only as a "white mongrel," was also decorated. He survived Afghanistan only to die back in London, under a cab, and was then stuffed and mounted at the regimental museum in England. Had he been a pensioner at the Royal Hospital Kilmainham, in any case, he would never have merited a spot alongside Vonolel. The Victorians were sticklers for breeding – and a canine mongrel could hardly be officer material. It doesn't seem like a coincidence that, even today, a sign at the entrance to the walled garden says: "No dogs allowed."

Address The Irish Museum of Modern Art, Military Road, Kilmainham, Dublin 8, Tel +353.(0)1.6129900, www.imma.ie | **Getting there** Bus routes 79, 79 a, or 145; or Luas Red Line to Heuston Station, then an 8-minute walk | **Hours** Tue–Fri 11.30am–5.30pm, Sat 10am–5.30pm, Sun noon–5.30pm. Admission free | **Tip** The horse is not buried under his relocated tombstone, by the way. His actual grave is in the middle of the gardens.

106 War Memorial Gardens
A memorial belatedly remembered

Officially a place of remembrance, the War Memorial Gardens at Islandbridge suffered a bad case of amnesia for much of the 20th century.

They commemorated a war, the 1914–18 one, that by its end had become both extremely unpopular and politically incorrect. As an independent Ireland emerged from the wreckage, memories of service to the British Empire were soon an embarrassment.

Designed by one of the greatest architects of his day, Edward Lutyens, the project started well. Despite the vast amount of digging and stone haulage required, it was done largely by hand, using pre-industrial techniques – partly as an act of homage, partly to create jobs in the depressed 1920s and 30s.

But this elaborate memorial to the "war to end all wars" was completed, ironically, in 1939. And by then most of Ireland, including the government, didn't want to know anything about it. Neglected, it gradually fell into dereliction, the fountains dry, the rose gardens wild, the stonework a blackboard for graffiti artists.

The gardens were restored in the 1980s, by which time Ireland was reclaiming even the parts of its history that didn't fit with the story of unrelenting struggle against colonial oppression. But the process wasn't complete until 2011, when Britain's Queen Elizabeth made a historic visit to the Republic, and as the scene of one of several ceremonies of reconciliation, Islandbridge lived up to its name.

Even today, however, the records at the garden's centre remain a secret to most Dubliners. Locked away (but opened on request) in two stone rooms are books listing the 49,400 Irishmen who died in the First World War, with their places of origin, rank and regiment, and the date and cause of death. The books are illustrated by Harry Clarke, an artist more famous for stained glass, but whose work for the war dead is also now benefitting from belated enlightenment.

Address Islandbridge, Dublin 8, Tel +353.(0)1.4757816, www.heritageireland.ie | **Getting there** Bus routes 51, 68, or 69; or Luas Red Line to Heuston Station, then a 10-minute walk | **Hours** Mon–Fri open at 8am, Sat & Sun open at 10am; closing times vary with daylight hours. Access to book rooms by appointment | **Tip** A short walk from the gardens, there are picnic tables overlooking the River Liffey and Islandbridge Weir.

107__Wellington Monument

An obelisk with a tall tale

There's a popular legend that in the early stages of the Wellington Monument's construction, a private dinner for subscribers was held in the vault underneath. The idea was to raise funds to continue the project, before – as part of the event's novelty – bricking up the vault, dinner table and all, as a kind of time capsule. And so it happened, according to the story.

Except that some time after the bricking up, it was noticed that a butler who had helped serve dinner was missing. Most versions of the tale go on to mention that the man had been well known for helping himself to the guests' wine between courses, leading to the terrible conclusion that he had been in a deep sleep somewhere at the end of the night when everybody else left.

The story is at least as tall as the obelisk, which rises to a European record 62 metres. But it probably serves a function in romanticising a structure that is otherwise inaccessible, in every sense. There are no stairs inside the tower, or outside, and no viewing platform. There's not even an explanatory note anywhere. It's just a giant, granite tribute to the Duke of Wellington. And like the man himself, it no longer inspires much affection in the country of his birth, which he himself considered a mere English colony.

It does, however, provoke a perennial argument: is the obelisk a monument or a testimonial? Pedants insist that monuments are for the dead, and that this is therefore a testimonial, since the duke was very much alive when building began in 1817. In fact, he was still alive when the project ran out of money a few years later, after which work was suspended for decades.

But by the time it was completed – several metres short of what was first planned – the duke was dead, like the phantom butler. So if anyone asks you, now you know. The obelisk is a testimonial and a monument, all in one.

Address Phoenix Park, Dublin 8 | Getting there Various bus routes, including 25 and 66 to Parkgate St, then a 10-minute walk; or Luas Red Line to Heuston Station, then a 15-minute walk | Hours Always open | Tip The brass reliefs on each side of the monument's base were made from a French cannon, melted down after the Battle of Waterloo.

108_ Wild Deer in Phoenix Park

A herd with a long history

The fallow deer herd that roams the Phoenix Park is as old as the 1752-acre enclosure itself. Not the individual animals, of course – the record age for one of those is 14. But the 450 or so deer currently making up the herd are direct descendants of the ones who roamed here in the 17th century, when this was designated a royal hunting park.

As befits their noble lineage, the deer still have the freedom of the place. In practice they spend most of their time in the "Fifteen Acres" (which is actually more like 200 acres), or the forested area to its north.

But they can turn up anywhere, as motorists on the park's main road occasionally find to their cost. Even when obeying the 50 kph speed limit, drivers need to be alert, especially at night. It's not unknown, either, for deer to make the occasional dash across the course during the park's many mass road-running events.

For the most part, they cohabit peacefully with the umpteen sports played around them, sharing the Fifteen Acres with football pitches and even model aeroplane enthusiasts. Dogs are a bigger worry. At the start of every summer, ubiquitous signs warn owners to keep them on a leash during fawning season.

Between 100 and 200 fawns can be born each year. And in fact, the deer breed too successfully at times. During the Second World War, when the population reached 1200 and resources were scarce, there was a major cull, reducing the herd to a mere 38. By 2005, it was back up to 800, and another cull was needed.

The deer are most popular with the public at Christmas, when Santa Claus appears daily to feed them. But enthusiasts watch them all year round, especially in June for the fawning, and in October's rutting season, when the antlered males provide their own sporting spectacle: locking horns with each other to establish supremacy.

Address Phoenix Park, Dublin 8 | **Getting there** Various bus routes to Parkgate St or Conyngham Rd, including 25, 25 a, 25 b, 26, 66, 66 a, 66 b, and 67; or Luas Red Line to Heuston Station | **Hours** Always open | **Tip** If viewing the deer, to save yourself a long walk, get a Dublin rental bike from Parkgate Street (free for the first 30 minutes; small but rising charges thereafter).

109 __Wittgenstein's Step

A refuge for one of the 20th century's great minds

The great Austrian philosopher Ludwig Wittgenstein was in the habit, when he needed to do some especially deep thinking, of travelling, in the words of one of his biographers, to the "most cold and desolate parts of Europe." He made such trips to Norway and Iceland. And it may have been in a similar spirit that he spent part of his later years in Ireland: in Connemara, Wicklow, and Dublin.

But it must have been a bit chillier in Dublin that he bargained for, because while there he became a frequent visitor to the Great Palm House of the National Botanic Gardens, where more tropical temperatures were guaranteed. He had resigned his teaching job at Cambridge University in 1947 to concentrate on writing. And sure enough, during the winter of 1948–49, he was noted for sitting on a stone step in the Botanic Gardens' Great Palm House making entries in his notebook for work that would be published posthumously. The step is today marked with a plaque.

The quiet of post-war Dublin was in stark contrast to Wittgenstein's turbulent life. Born the same week as Adolf Hitler, he also attended the same school, but was two years ahead of the future dictator, because Hitler was forced to repeat a year, while the ultra-intelligent Wittgenstein skipped one.

But the philosopher was also dogged for much of his life by the mental depression that ran in his family. Three of his brothers took their own lives. And while in Dublin, Wittgenstein also made a habit of visiting St Patrick's psychiatric hospital and talking at length to the patients there, including one elderly man who was said to be more intelligent than any of his doctors.

Apart from its contribution to his writings, the stay in Ireland may have helped Wittgenstein's frame of mind. His later years were happier than his early ones. When he died from prostate cancer in Cambridge, in 1951, his parting words were: "Tell them I had a wonderful life."

Address National Botanic Gardens, Glasnevin, Dublin 9, Tel +353.(0)1.8570909, www.botanicgardens.ie | **Getting there** Bus routes 4, 9, 13, or 83 | **Hours** Mar–Oct, Mon–Fri 9am–5pm, Sat & Sun 10am–6pm; Nov–Feb, Mon–Fri 9am–4.30pm, Sat & Sun 10am–4.30pm | **Tip** Since 2013, for the first time in two centuries, the Botanic Gardens and its historic neighbour, Glasnevin Cemetery, have been linked by a pedestrian entrance. This saves a 15-minute walk and, along with Tolka Valley Park, creates a continuous green space of more than 200 acres, Dublin's second largest after Phoenix Park.

110___The Wonderful Barn

An otherworldly wonder of 18th-century architecture

Leixlip is not in Dublin, strictly speaking – not even Greater Dublin. It's just across the county boundary, in Kildare. But it's very much part of the commuter belt: a mere 45 minutes from the city centre on the No 67 bus. And it might just be worth the trip there to visit one of the weirder buildings you'll ever see.

The Wonderful Barn was erected in 1743, primarily as a famine relief scheme to give employment to workers in hard times. It's also a classic "folly": an architectural fantasy commissioned by the estate owners to provide a visual focus to the east of Castletown House.

Tapering up to a height of 24 metres, with the stairs on the outside and a crow's nest viewing space on top, it doesn't look very practical. But it did, apparently, serve as a real barn, hence the hole at the centre of each of its floors. Other theories are that it may have been used as a dovecote – its design is echoed by two smaller dovecotes nearby – and/or, conversely, as a place from which to shoot game.

Unfortunately, it's not in a very good state these days, and the neglect extends to the surrounding buildings. The hope is that concerned groups, including the National Heritage Council and the Irish Georgian Society, will find a new use for it, sooner or later.

In the meantime, you can at least visit the structure and marvel at it, for free. Having done that, you can also visit Castletown House, built between 1722 and 1729 for William Conolly, then Speaker of the Irish House of Commons and, outside the aristocracy, Ireland's wealthiest man. Now in state ownership, Castletown was the country's first Palladian-style mansion, and remains the largest. Among its impressed visitors over the centuries was the English aristocrat Richard Twiss, who toured the area in 1775 and commented: "This is I believe the only house in Ireland to which the term palace can be applied."

Address Celbridge Road, Leixlip, County Kildare, Tel +353.(0)1.6288252, www.castletown.ie | Getting there Bus route 67 | Hours Castletown estate's opening times vary from month to month. Access to the house is by guided tour Mon–Sat, starting at 10.15am and then on the hour from 11am–5pm. Sun guided tours at 10.15am, 11am, & 5pm; self-guided tours noon–4.45pm | Tip A smaller, less well-constructed version of the Wonderful Barn can be seen in Rathfarnham, Dublin. There, it's called the "Bottle Tower."

111__Ye Olde Hurdy-Gurdy Museum of Vintage Radio

One man's passion, now an exhibition

On the outside, it's just another of the Martello towers that line the coast of Dublin, left over from the Napoleonic panic of the early 1800s. Inside, it holds an astonishing trove of old radios, gramophones, and TVs, amounting to a chaotic but fascinating history of 20th-century broadcasting.

The museum began as the personal collection of Pat Herbert, a radio enthusiast whose home was gradually overtaken by his hobby until, mercifully, Fingal County Council offered him use of the refurbished tower in 2003. It was an apt venue. In the early days of radio, the same building had played host to the experiments of Guglielmo Marconi, the Italian who pioneered long-distance transmission, and of a U.S. rival, Lee de Forest. Both were sending communications across the sea to Wales. And the suspicion is that the greater promise of de Forest's work was not rewarded because British establishment figures had invested in Marconi's company. In any case, each man contributed to the rapid development of broadcasting, of which the museum suggests the dizzying pace.

Exhibits range from an ancient Edison phonograph to a late-20th-century vinyl LP played by the repeated revolutions of a toy minibus. Another favourite is a French wartime radio, disguised as a framed portrait of Rita Hayworth until you flip it over (which it was hoped visiting German troops wouldn't do) and find a receiver in the back.

Also from that era is a Pye Radio cabinet with an Art Deco design featuring a sun rising. Originally, it rose through clouds, and sold well. But post-war, somebody thought it would be a good idea to lose the clouds. Unfortunately, it then looked like the Japanese flag. Sales in the States nosedived. Most sets had to be destroyed.

Address 6 Balscadden Road, Howth, County Dublin, Tel +353.(0)86.8154189, hurdygurdyradiomuseum.wordpress.com | Getting there DART rail to Howth, then a 10-minute walk; or bus routes 31 or 31a | Hours May–Oct, daily 11am–4pm; Nov–Apr, Sat & Sun 11am–4pm. Admission: €5 for adults, children free | Tip The museum's name comes from a quotation by the then Irish Taoiseach (prime minister), describing early radio as "the old hurdy-gurdy."

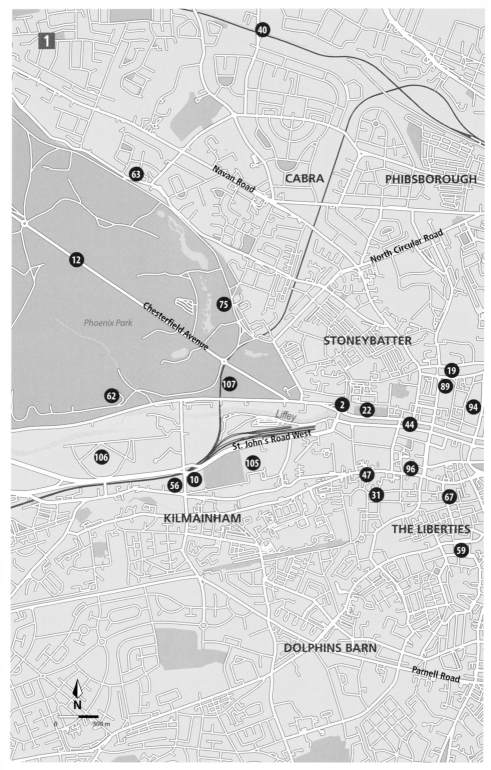

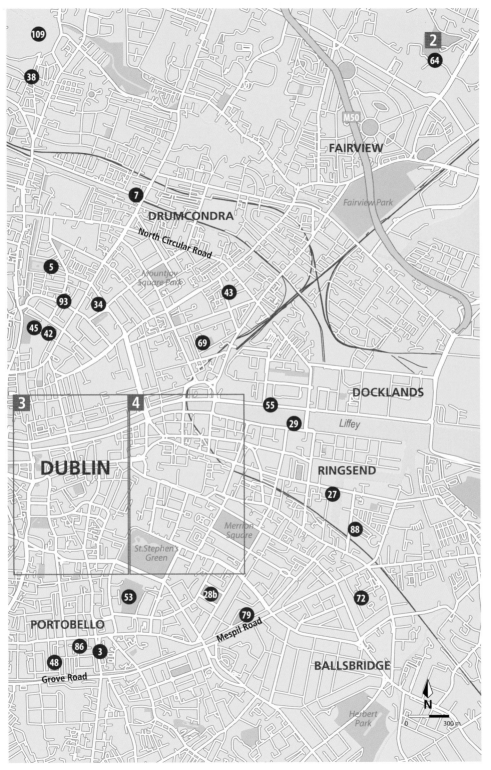

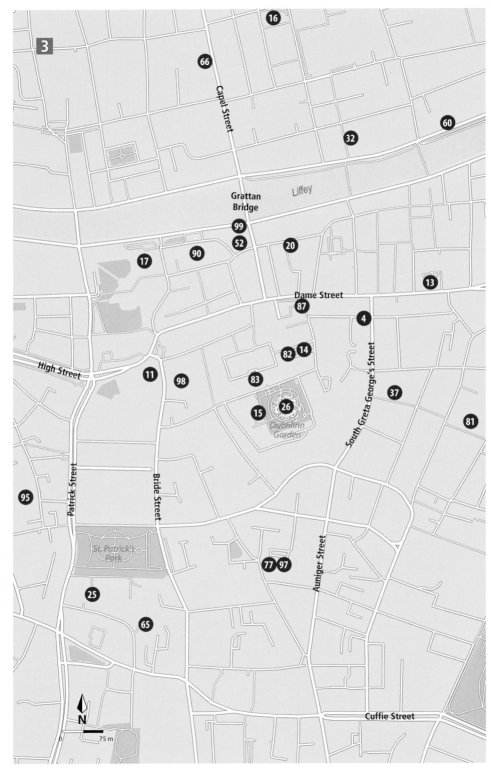

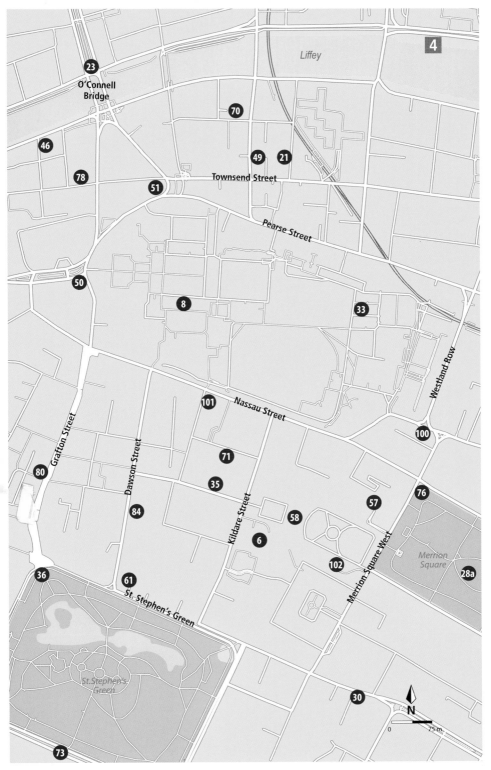

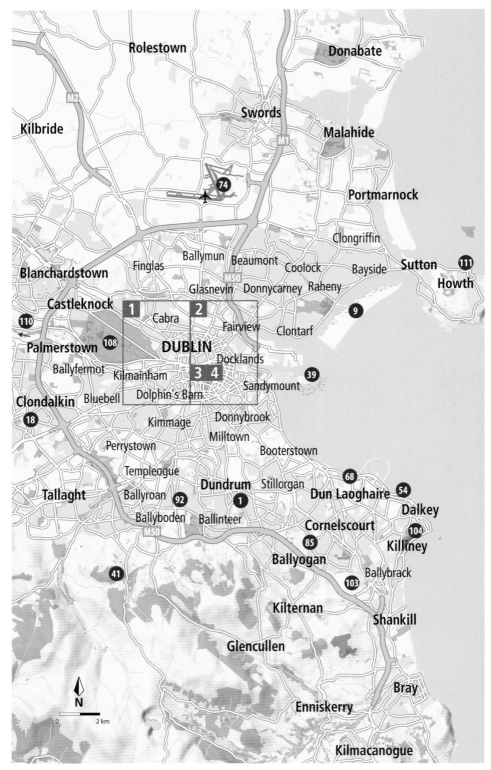

Lucia Jay von Seldeneck,
Carolin Huder, Verena Eidel
**111 PLACES IN BERLIN
THAT YOU SHOULDN'T MISS**
ISBN 978-3-95451-208-9

Rüdiger Liedtke
**111 PLACES IN MUNICH
THAT YOU SHOULDN'T MISS**
ISBN 978-3-95451-222-5

John Sykes
**111 PLACES IN LONDON
THAT YOU SHOULDN'T MISS**
ISBN 978-3-95451-346-8

Rike Wolf
**111 PLACES IN HAMBURG
THAT YOU SHOULDN'T MISS**
ISBN 978-3-95451-234-8

Paul Kohl
**111 PLACES IN BERLIN
ON THE TRAIL OF THE NAZIS**
ISBN 978-3-95451-323-9

Peter Eickhoff
**111 PLACES IN VIENNA
THAT YOU SHOULDN'T MISS**
ISBN 978-3-95451-206-5

Sharon Fernandes
**111 Places In New Delhi
That You Must Not Miss**
ISBN 978-3-95451-648-3

Sally Asher, Michael Murphy
**111 Places In New Orleans
That You Must Not Miss**
ISBN 978-3-95451-645-2

Gordon Streisand
**111 Places In Miami
And The Keys
That You Must Not Miss**
ISBN 978-3-95451-644-5

Dirk Engelhardt
**111 PLACES IN BARCELONA
THAT YOU MUST NOT MISS**
ISBN 978-3-95451-353-6

Rüdiger Liedtke
**111 PLACES ON MALLORCA
THAT YOU SHOULDN'T MISS**
ISBN 978-3-95451-281-2

Marcus X. Schmid
**111 PLACES IN ISTANBUL
THAT YOU MUST NOT MISS**
ISBN 978-3-95451-423-6

Stefan Spath
**111 PLACES IN SALZBURG
THAT YOU SHOULDN'T MISS**
ISBN 978-3-95451-230-0

Ralf Nestmeyer
**111 PLACES IN PROVENCE
THAT YOU MUST NOT MISS**
ISBN 978-3-95451-422-9

Christiane Bröcker,
Babette Schröder
**111 PLACES IN STOCKHOLM
THAT YOU MUST NOT MISS**
ISBN 978-3-95451-459-5

Beate C. Kirchner
**111 Places in Florence
and Northern Tuscany
That You Must Not Miss**
ISBN 978-3-95451-613-1

Floriana Petersen, Steve Werney
**111 Places in San Francisco
That You Must Not Miss**
ISBN 978-3-95451-609-4

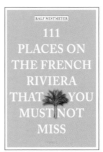

Ralf Nestmeyer
**111 Places on the
French Riviera
That You Must Not Miss**
ISBN 978-3-95451-612-4

Gerd Wolfgang Sievers
111 PLACES IN VENICE
THAT YOU MUST NOT MISS
ISBN 978-3-95451-460-1

Petra Sophia Zimmermann
111 PLACES IN VERONA
AND LAKE GARDA THAT
YOU MUST NOT MISS
ISBN 978-3-95451-611-7

Rüdiger Liedtke,
Laszlo Trankovits
111 Places in Cape Town
That You Must Not Miss
ISBN 978-3-95451-610-0

Annett Klingner
111 PLACES IN ROME
THAT YOU MUST NOT MISS
ISBN 978-3-95451-469-4

Jo-Anne Elikann
111 PLACES IN NEW YORK
THAT YOU MUST NOT MISS
ISBN 978-3-95451-052-8

Giulia Castelli Gattinara,
Mario Verin
111 Places in Milan
That You Must Not Miss
ISBN 978-3-95451-331-4

Mark Gabor, Susan Lusk
111 SHOPS IN NEW YORK
THAT YOU MUST NOT MISS
ISBN 978-3-95451-351-2

Kirstin von Glasow
111 SHOPS IN LONDON
THAT YOU SHOULDN'T MISS
ISBN 978-3-95451-341-3

Kirstin von Glasow
111 COFFEESHOPS IN LONDON
THAT YOU MUST NOT MISS
ISBN 978-3-95451-614-8

The Author

Frank McNally is a newspaper reporter and columnist. Born in County Monaghan, near the Irish border, he moved to Dublin in his late teens, working for a number of government departments. He later studied journalism at Dublin City University and in 1996 joined the staff of the *Irish Times*, where he is now the Chief Writer of the daily column "An Irishman's Diary."

The Photographer

Róisín McNally was born and raised in Dublin and grew up visiting many of the lesser-known places featured in this book at the heels of her adventurous father. She is currently studying at the Institute of Education in Dublin.